DIY PROJECTS

LANDSCAPING

HOW TO DESIGN YOUR OWN LANDSCAPE

JOHANNES POULARD

DIY PROJECTS: LANDSCAPING: HOW TO DESIGN YOUR OWN LANDSCAPE

For do-it-yourselfers who want a professional quality landscaped yard all year round

INTRODUCTION:

Have you ever thought you spent too much money on your landscaping. Though in years past, people mowed their own lawns and trimmed their own bushes, today landscape maintenance and design is a multimillion dollar business. People today spend millions of dollars on not only materials to do their landscape design but to hire professionals to do it.

The whole idea of How to Design your Own Landscape is to give you the tools and the tricks to do a professional job on your own yard and not pay the professional price.

Written by professional landscapers who have been in the industry for more than ten years, this book is a full in-depth guide on how to do everything in your yard yourself, from planting flowers and lawn maintenance to water gardening and proper pond maintenance.

When reading this book, you will learn all the skills to properly mix both concrete and mortar, learn the names and uses of the proper masonry tools which you can use for building your own masonry walls and features from either brick or natural stone. You will also learn about how to do stonework using the dry stack method without any mortaring.

You will also learn about proper lawn seeding and mowing. The most important thing, however, where all do-it-yourselfers make the biggest mistakes is fertilizing your lawn. You will understand the difference between chemical and organic fertilizers. You will also understand that there are different procedures when it comes to the two fertilizers.

Uneven pavers are probably the most annoying thing in your walks or patios. In How to Design your Own Landscape, you will also learn the different packing media available, the benefits of both mason sand and moon dust as a bed for your paver bricks. You will also learn how to properly set up the area you want paved and how to tamp the pavers into place so they are even.

Why pay several hundred dollars to have a concrete truck come in and pour a slab of concrete? Well, if you need to pour a small slab of concrete, you will learn how to properly mix concrete, what goes into concrete and when learning about concrete and mortar, you will learn what Portland cement is and the different letter codes which denote how much Portland cement is in the cement mix you want to use. You will also learn for which type of cementing the different letter codes are meant for.

If you are a do-it-yourselfer and want to have a professional quality job, or are just a beginner, just bought a house, but don't want to spend money on a contractor, then this book is good reading material for you.

Table of Contents

Chapter Tree: Choosing and controlling ground cover, different varieties of ground cover plants, preventing ground cover from growing in areas where they are not intended to grow.

Chapter Four: Proper lawn maintenance in summer and fall. Maintenance of your lawnmower, why leaves are bad for your lawn, proper fertilization of your lawn, and winterization.

Chapter Five: Paving and creating paths — Learn how to properly install paver bricks or stones, using packing material, such as packing sand and moon dust. Use of pea gravel, road pack, and river rock.

Chapter Six: Enhance your landscaping with stonework. Learn different kinds of stonework, dry stack and masonry, proper mortar mixing. Denoting mortar strength codes, building landscape features for your front and back yard using stone masonry, such as grills, fire pits, and sitting areas.

Chapter Seven: Water gardening and water features. Turn your backyard into your private sanctuary. Learn how to build ponds using both loose stone and masonry, different water features, hardscaping, building water manifolds to control water features, stocking fish, types of pond fish, pond plants, proper filtration, biological treatment, and winterization.

Epilogue: How to employ all the skills covered in the above chapters to create your own personal landscaping like a pro.

Chapter One

Basic Landscape Design and Installation

Do you have a lousy or just unattractive yard? Don't have the money to hire a professional landscaper to create that curb appeal and a great backyard, which you can enjoy for ages to come. Well, this book is for people who like to do things around the yard themselves. In this chapter, you will learn about the following:

A. **Basic landscape design:** how to properly compose your yard with the use of your computer or on paper.
B. **Proper planting of trees, shrubs, annuals, and perennials:** organic fertilizers versus chemical fertilizers, mixing planting soil with peat moss, and preventing your flower beds from being overtaken by weeds.
C. **Positioning sprinklers and creating an in-ground sprinkler system:** Creating your own irrigation solutions from items you can purchase at your local home improvement store.
D. **Proper lawn planting:** using both sod or seeding. Different types of grass and what is good for sunny or shady yards.

Basic Landscape Design
Before you can have a nice yard to enjoy during the summer, or the other three seasons, you need to design your landscape. If you are a good artist and can draw, you can draw your design on paper, but using special architectural software to design your yard properly.

Landscape design software packages are readily available in many home improvement stores. One caveat, however, you want to make sure you have a good quality program for your computer before you purchase a software package. The period we currently live in is digital and we have easy access to digital cameras. Many of you own smartphones with a high quality digital camera built in. That's all you need, if you have a good home design software package.

A good quality landscape design software package will allow you to import photos from your digital camera of your home and yard. You can then manipulate these photos within the program by adding flowers, features, and other things you would like to have in your landscape design.

Good landscape design programs may also use the internet to give you access to the USDA zone your home is located in. This is definitely a plus, as certain plants can be perennials in different USDA zones further south, yet those same plants can only grow as annuals in other USDA zones. The USDA has created a special growing map of the United States, which is divided in different zones with color codes ranging from blues to yellows and reds. The more blue your zone is, the colder your climate is. Vis versa, the more yellow or red your zone is, the warmer your climate is.

Some landscape design programs will actually have the USDA climate zone map with thousands of plants which are compatible for each zone. A good landscape design program should also give you information about the different plants, whether they will grow in your climate zone as perennials or annuals.

Choosing the right landscape design software for your computer can be a bit tricky. There are many programs which are compatible with both Windows or MAC OS. You need to know what operating system your computer runs on. Today, most macs are outfitted with either the Maverix or Yosemite OS. Older macs which still run Mountain Lion may not be compatible with programs sold today, so you may want to upgrade your mac. With PCs, the same thing is true. Most software sold in stores today are made for the latest versions of Windows, so if you have an older PC which runs on Windows XP, 2000, etc, you may want to consider upgrading, otherwise your software may not work properly.

When choosing your landscape design software, follow these simple tips so you can create your own professional quality landscape design plan properly without any glitches.

A. **What operating system** is the software compatible with. If you are not familiar with what kind of operating system your computer runs on, contact someone you know who is tech savvy or have him come with you to buy your software.
B. **What are the storage and RAM requirements** for the software you are planning on buying. Many landscape design software packages do run many high resolution graphics, so they can be fairly large thus they may require large RAM and storage to run. Again if you are not tech savvy, have a friend who is look at your computer and come with you when you buy the software.
C. **Installing the software** should be fairly simple. For mac users, the software should install fairly easily. Windows users may need to follow an install wizard, thus if you are not tech savvy, have a tech savvy friend help you install the software.

Following these simple instructions when choosing your landscape design software, you should be able to use it and design the yard of your dreams.

Features to use in your landscape design software are also important. After you have imported the photos of your yard, doing the design, and making your layout, you should print the layout on paper. Many of these layouts are too large for basic legal size printer paper, so you need to tile the parts of the layout and tape them together. If you use a laptop, you can go to a print shop, such as Kinkos, or similar store and plug your computer into one of their professional printers to print out the full layout. The cost is minimal and can usually be done. Many of these publishing stores do have staff who can help you print your layout out.

Landscape calculator is a feature which most home and landscape design programs have. They may have a different name, but this is a handy feature as it can help you calculate how many materials, flowers, shrubs, and trees you will need along with a ballpark cost of the project.

Proper Planting of Trees, Shrubs, Perennials, and Annuals
What kind of landscape design comes without trees, shrubs, perennials, and annuals? None, basically, unless you like simple rock gardens. Even rock gardens have some plants. Thus the proper planting of them will ensure the plants thrive in your creation.

Trees and shrubs are probably the most difficult things to plant. The best time to plant these is in the spring before the sap starts to run or in the fall after the first frost. During this period, most trees and shrubs are dormant and have a better chance of surviving. You can plant trees and evergreens in the middle of summer also, but you will have to water them on a regular basis.

Basic tips on planting trees and shrubs safely and successfully are listed below. If you follow these tips, your trees may suffer some shock, which is to be expected, but will bounce back quickly and grow and flourish the next year.

A. **Dig a hole twice the size of the root ball.** Whenever you buy a tree for planting, the roots are tied up in a root ball. The root ball protects the roots of the tree by keeping them moist while being transported. The root ball usually wraps the roots of the tree or shrub in natural burlap and bound with either hemp twine or metal wire. Never buy a tree with a root ball wrapped in plastic. See figure one to get the idea of how the hole needs to be dug.

B. **Have a garden hose with a constant stream of running water** go into the hole where you are planting your tree or shrub.Newly planted trees require a lot of water to allow the sap to run. It is a natural defense of a tree or shrub to stop running sap when uprooted to prevent the core of the tree from dying.

C. **Have good quality planting soil and peat moss** available in proportion to the hole for the tree or shrub you are planting. This is why a hole should be twice the size of the root ball. Most areas, soil is not adequate to provide enough nutrients for for the newly planted tree or shrub. Thus you should mix an even 50/50 mix of good black soil with peat moss to fill up half the hole as you place the tree in it.

D. **Untie the root ball** before planting the tree or shrub. Most trees and shrubs have their roots planted in clay soil, as it maintains moisture and is easy to keep from falling apart. Using a sharp but rugged knife, cut the burlap and hemp twine. If the root ball is tied with metal wire, use a good pair of wire cutters to cut the wire. There is no need to remove all the burlap. Most burlap is made from hemp, like natural rope, thus it will decay in the ground. Simply cut holes in the burlap and loose the clay soil pack underneath the burlap. Cut all the bindings. This allows the roots to expand and grow out of the ball and reach the natural water table. Keep the water running as you plant the tree or shrub.

E. **Close the hole** with the remaining dirt after fertilizing the root ball and make a dirt wall around the base of the trunk. The dirt wall forms a bowl which will channel the water to the roots of the newly planted tree or shrub. Be sure the crown is not covered with any dirt. If the crown gets covered, it can cause rot, which will kill the tree or shrub. The crown is the base of the trunk where the roots grow from and is naturally exposed to the elements.

F. **Have a soaker hose** running constantly for the first two weeks after planting unless there is a lot of rain. The soaker hose controls the water flow and soaks the soil without washing out the dirt wall. Be sure your tree is then watered on a regular basis for the rest of the season. Trees and shrubs usually take a year before they are fully established in their new environment.

When using fertilizers, you can be bombarded with different types of fertilizers, both organic and chemical. Though there are success stories with chemical fertilizers, organic fertilizers are by far the best way to go. Check with your local nursery to see what they recommend.

Figure One: digging the hole for a tree or shrub

Planting Perennials

Perennials are flowers which grow back and flower every year without having to replace them. Planting perennials can be a bit tricky. It is recommended that you start your landscape design a year before completion. There are thousands of perennials around for planting, but when they need to be planted depends on whether they have tubers, bulbs, or roots. Many larger lilies and other like flowers can be planted in the summer out of pots and are sold regularly at many nurseries and home improvement stores during their flowering seasons. Others need to be planted in the fall or spring. We suggest that you place steaks with a marked label in areas where you plan to plant different perennials which grow at different times of the year.

Common types of perennials along with when and how they are planted are listed below. These perennials may be considered annuals in colder climates, check the USDA map to make sure.

A. **Narcissus** flower in early spring, from March to early May. In warmer states, such as Florida and southern Texas, they may flower in late February to early April. Narcissus are very common spring perennials in many landscapes. Daffodils and jonquils are both in the narcissus genus. These need a hard freeze to flower, thus they should be planted in the fall. Typically, the narcissus bulbs are planted from late September in Canada to late November in Florida. Typically, most of the lower 48 of the United States, narcissus bulbs should be planted in October. Simply dig a hole with a garden trowel or special bulb planter, place the bulb upright and add a mix of bulb fertilizer and bonemeal, cover with dirt.

B. **Tulips** are also common perennials which come in multiple colors ranging from deep bright reds to beautiful whites to variegated pedals and flower from early to mid spring. These are also bulb perennials and are planted like and during the same times of the year as narcissus bulbs.

C. **Hyacinths** are also a bulb perennial and flower in early to mid spring. These flower with a clustered group of small flowers with colors ranging from blues, reds, purples, pinks, and whites. Hyacinth bulbs are planted like and during the same times of the year as narcissus and tulip bulbs.

D. **Hostas** are a very common perennial which can give beautiful green leafy decor to your summer landscape. These are also very low maintenance and come in a wide variety of genus. Hostas can be solid color leaves with different shades of greens to dark blues and variegated with white or yellow with the green. Some hostas are small and make a great border for your lawn or flowerbed, whereas others are very large and can be great center pieces in your perennial flower arrangements. Hostas can be planted anytime during the summer months. Hostas grow out of a tuber and they do multiply quickly. They can get large, so you may need to divide them occasionally. Hostas can be expensive, especially some of the larger varieties, thus if you have a friend who has large hostas, ask if you can divide theirs and get them for free. Hostas are ideal for gardens with a lot of shade.

E. **Day lilies** usually flower during the summer months. Typically they can be planted when they bloom. Most nurseries and stores which sell home and garden merchandise will sell day lilies in pots and can be planted in your flower beds. Day lilies do need sun. Day lilies have many hybrids with a wide variety of colors and shapes.

F. **Tiger lilies** flower in late summer. These perennials grow very tall stalks and have an orange flower. In most of the lower 48 states of the US, they bloom from mid August to early September. Very easy to plant. Remove from pot and plant with fertilizer and planting soil.

G. **Peonese** are perennials wich have a red to white rose like flower and bloom in May and June. They are typically planted when they either bloom or are about to bloom. You can buy them in their pots and plant them during their flowering season.

H. **Coleus (Florida only)** are perennials in Florida only. These can be grown as annuals in other parts of the US. Coleus are in the mint family and come in a wide variety of hybrids with multiple colored leaves. These plants are mainly grown for their colorful foliage and typically do not have an attractive flower. Many people cut off the flower to allow the coleus to grow into large bushes. Florida and Hawaii are the only states where the climate is warm enough for coleus to grow as a perennial and can grow so large, many people who live in these two states grow them as colorful hedges.

I. **Impatients (Florida only)**, like coleus, are only perennials in Florida and Hawaii. They are grown as annuals in the greater lower 48 states of the US, but there are different varieties which can grow as large green hedges with flowers which can be any color from red to pink to white.

J. **Ornamental grasses** are ideal for areas which have lots of sunlight and have a dry sandy soil. They are low maintenance and the larger varieties of ornamental grasses need to have their dead stalks and thatch removed in late fall or early spring to allow for the new grass to come up. Ornamental grasses typically do not flower, but will have fluffy plumes in late summer.

K. **Ferns** are a tuber perennial and favor more shady areas. They can be planted much like hostas, but are a bit more temperamental and have more difficulties to establish themselves. When planting ferns, do not expect them to grow big and full after planting. They will die, but come back the following year.

There are many different varieties of perennials around and more than can be possibly mentioned in one chapter, thus research the kinds of perennials you want to have in your landscape.

Planting Annuals

Annuals are flowers which need to be replanted every year. Most annuals are planted in early summer and typically die off after the first frost. Though some annuals can be perennials in warmer climates, such as coleus and impatients, which are grown as large hedges in Florida and Hawaii, where frosts are not as frequent as in other parts of North America. The reason most people plant annuals is primarily to add color to their flower gardens and landscapes during the summer months. Many annuals favor shady areas, though there are a few which require sun. Annuals are great to add color to flowerbeds, planters, hanging baskets, or flower boxes in front of the windows. Common annuals are listed below.

A. **Coleus** are a very popular annual for yards which have a lot of shade. They are very easy to grow and can easily be propagated. A member of the mint family, coleus are typically grown for their colorful foliage. Unless you are in Florida or Hawaii, where coleus can keep growing and get large enough to be hedges, they are ideal for color accenting in flowerbeds, planters, and other places. Coleus do not survive hard freezes, thus if you want to have large coleus, you need to bring them in for the winter. Because coleus are considered a subtropical plant, they will not flourish well in winter sunlight, so if you want to grow them year round and have them get bigger, you should get some growth lamps. Propagation is easy. Simply take rooting powder and wet mason sand. Cut a section of your favorite coleus off and place the cut end in the rooting powder and place in wet mason sand pot. Within two weeks, check if there are roots growing and plant in potting soil. They will grow and you can have a summer yard which is the envy of the block. Coleus need to be watered on a regular basis.

B. **Impatients** are another popular annual. Like coleus, they are also considered a subtropical perennial and will not survive a hard freeze. Impatients are typically a shade annual with the exception of the New Zealand impatients, which like sunlight. Different impatient varieties are listed below. All impatients need to be watered on a regular basis.

    1. **Common impatients** have green heart shaped leaves and are constantly producing small clover shaped flowers which can be red, white, salmon, or pink. Great for hanging baskets, potted plants, or planters in shady to semi-shady areas in your yard. Impatients can be propagated like coleus, but they can take more time to grow roots and get established.

    2. **Double impatients** are similar to common impatients. They have heart shaped leaves, they constantly produce flowers all summer and have the same colors as common impatients. The difference is that double impatients have a more rose like look than the common impatients.

    3. **New Zealand impatients** like semi-shade to full sun and are the more expensive variety of impatients. These have rose like flowers, like double impatients, but are much larger. New Zealand impatients typically flower bright deep reds and have dark green pointy leaves. Great for flower boxes by windows and planters.

C. **Begonias** are annuals which like semi-shade to full sun. Typically, begonias have leaves which are variegated from green to a dark burgundy to red. Begonias have small white or red flowers. They make great border plants. Begonias need to be watered daily

D. **Marigolds** are small single stem flowers with a yellow and orange ball blossom. They like full sun and are known to keep mosquitos away. Marigolds can be planted in either shade or sun and need moderate watering.

E. **Petunias** are typically good for hanging baskets. These like full sun and can have flowers in a wide variety of color. Petunias need ample watering.

There are many annuals you can get and come late May to early June, many stores and nurseries will have annuals available in flats, pots, or hanging baskets. If you are looking to plant annuals in your flowerbeds, you would be better off buying them by the flat. A flat is a plastic rectangular tray which carries deeper trays with six seedlings in each section tray. These plastic sections which can be removed from the flat are made to easily tear the seedling out and plant in your flowerbed. Potted annuals are ideal for planters and hanging baskets.

Keeping your flowerbeds from being overtaken by weeds can be done by placing weed barrier down under the mulch. Use only fiber weed barrier. It is strong and allows the soil to breathe. Plastic can cause soil to stay moist and allow for the growth of fungi which can be harmful to your plants. Most fibrous weed barrier is made from a heavy duty nylon mesh which does not allow for weeds to take root in the soil. Simply steak out where you plant what and cut holes in those areas. Then once the weed barrier is down and securely anchored, spread a hefty layer of mulch several inches thick. This will help retain needed moisture and provide nutrients for your plants. Though mulch begins to decay and turns into soil at the bottom, weeds may seed themselves, but their roots will not be able to penetrate the barrier, so they can easily be pulled out.

Irrigation

Any landscape design with lawns and plants require a good irrigation system. Any home improvement store will have garden hoses, adapters for water spickets, and sprinklers available. You can also get timers which run on batteries to turn your sprinklers on at different times of the day. Typically, during the heat of mid summer, watering should only be done early in the morning or early evening. Watering in the middle of the day can shock your plants and kill them, especially if you have a lot of sun.

Use of sprinklers for your lawn or flowers can depend on what kind of irrigation system you have. If you are using basic garden hoses, a timer for your lawns is ideal, but some flowers need to be watered more gently. For lawns, ideal sprinklers can be a large fan sprinkler which lets the water spray fan out and the sprayer osculates back and forth. A swivel sprinkler is also great for your lawn, especially if you have large lawns. A swivel sprinkler makes the classic sprinkler sound and will rotate while shooting out large jet streams of water, giving maximum coverage to your lawn. Flowers are more delicate and a softer and gentle rain sprinkler is ideal for watering annuals and perennials.

The DIY in-ground sprinkler system can be a way to eliminate that pesky hose which is always in the way, has to be moved when the lawn needs mowing, etc. The DIY sprinkler system should only be built where you have good water pressure, as it works on professional sprinklers and underground sprinkler pipe. The steps for creating a DIY in-ground sprinkler system are as follows:

A. **Any major home improvement warehouse store,** such as Lowe's or Home Depot will have a whole section on in ground sprinkler systems. After careful planning, purchase the amount of underground irrigation piping and sprinkler heads for the areas in your yard which need watering.
B. **At the plumbing section** purchase PVC piping, bead joints and elbow joints, PVC cement, and hose spicket adapters. Then from the seasonal or garden section, get a garden hose timer and some length of garden hose.
C. **Dig a trench** about one and a half to two inches deep where the underground sprinkler pipe is supposed to go. Underground sprinkler pipe is typically made from a flexible form of PVC

and is a quarter inch in diameter. Make sure the sprinkler heads are vertical and up right to avoid compromising water output.

D. Near the hose spicket use the PVC pipe fittings to attach the garden hose to the pipe and the underground sprinkler pipe on the other end.

E. Burry everything once you feel it is installed correctly. Test everything to check if you need to make any adjustments.

When building your DIY in-ground sprinkler system, you want to make sure you do this before planting your lawn. Be sure your sprinkler heads are a bit above the ground, as once the dirt or sod is in place for your lawn it will be at the right level. See Figures Two to Five for a visual aid on how this is to be built.

Figure Two Sprinkler system layout

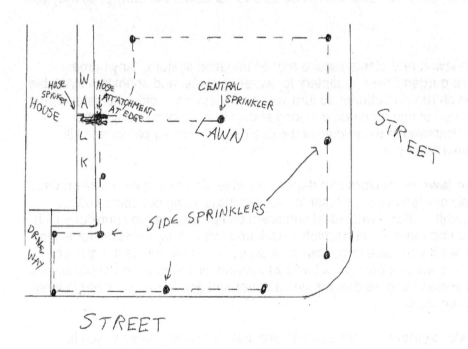

Figure   **Three** Garden hose and PVC fitting for spicket

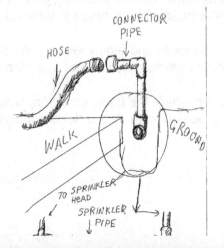

Figure Four Proper positioning of sprinkler heads

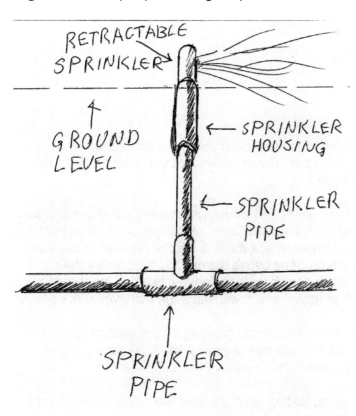

Figure Five How system operates in ideal conditions

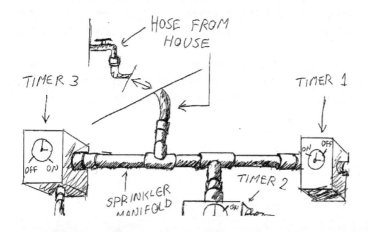

Note that all the timers on the manifold are set to turn on and off at different times. This is specifically recommended to maintain good water pressure at all times.

Proper Lawn Planting

One of the biggest frustrations of DIY landscapers is not having the grass grow properly. Many people think that grass is difficult to grow, but it's not. If you know what you are doing, you can have a green lawn which is the envy of the block.

Preparing the ground for the lawn is very important. As a rule, grass does not like acidic soil. This is why it can be difficult to grow a stellar lawn in certain parts of the United States. For example, in the Great Lakes region and other areas where there is a large number of oaks and pines, the soil can be too acidic as oaks and pine trees cause the soil to be acidic by their shedding leaves and needles. The acidic soil and thick leathery leaves, like oak leaves, can cake on the ground and allow for the growth of moss, which will make the soil even more acidic.

Moss is your lawn's main arch enemy. Where there is moss growing on the ground, grass will not grow. Even the spores of the moss will kill any attempt to grow a lawn. Typically, moss likes very shady areas, thus lawns are more successful in sunny areas.

The basic steps in preparing your yard for a long lasting lawn are covered below. This should be followed for both the laying of sod and seeding.

A. **Inspect the area** where you want your lawn. You want to make sure that it is moss free. If you spot moss or patches of moss, then you need to kill the moss spores. You should first scrape the visible moss from the surface of your lawn area. Then you will want to go to the garden center near you and ask what they have as an effective agent to kill off any moss spores. Note that some fungi, primarily garden mushrooms with no edible value, can leave spores which can kill your lawn too. Ideally, you will want to get an agent which is not only an anti-moss agent, but doubles as an anti-fungal agent as well. These agents can either be sold as a powder which can be spread with a lawn spreader or in a sprayer and mixed with water from your garden hose.

B. **Take a Ph test of the soil** in your lawn area. Chances are that if you live in an area where lawns are difficult to maintain and many people struggle to keep a well manicured lawn, the soil is very acidic. If your Ph level is from 1 to 4, then the soil is very acidic. 5 to 8 is considered to be neutral and 9 to 14 is alkaline. In general grass varieties used in lawns like a more alkaline soil, so you want to get the soil less acidic and more alkaline. Acidity can be managed by applying lime to the ground. You will want to spread the lime in your lawn spreader and then mix it with new soil.

C. **Before planting** you want to make sure that you can calculate how many yards of top soil you will need to plant your new lawn. You want to get a nutrient rich top soil which has lime and fertilizer in it. You should spread a two to three inch blanket of top soil before planting any grass.

Sod is the quickest way to get your lawn and make it ready for the whole family. Basically, sod is a grass carpet. It gets delivered to you as rolls of dirt with grass on one side. The soil which has the grass roots are usually bound together with a netting. Simply unroll each section of sod and make each section but up against each other. Cut the sod sections around the edges of your lawn. Water regularly. Sod establishes quickly and requires less maintenance than seed.

Seeding can be challenging, but the biggest problem is keeping the birds away. Birds are attracted to grass seed, as it is an easy meal. When seeding grass, you will want to have a special liquid fertilizer which mixes with water from your garden hose in a sprayer. You will want to water the seed with this fertilizer mix for several weeks until grass gets thick and green. Grass seed tends to sprout within a week of being spread. Make sure you choose a good fertilizer which also has a special agent which makes the flavor of the seeds unpleasant to birds.

When growing your lawn, you will also want to have an agent which can work into the soil to kill any grubs or other insects which can attract moles.

Installation is the longest part of your project. Once your landscape design is complete, with some maintenance, you can have the envy of the block.

Chapter Two

Basic Care of Landscape Trees and Shrubs

Many of you who want to do your own landscape design probably want some decorative landscape trees and shrubs to add focal points to your curb appeal. There is a wide variety of different landscape trees and shrubs, ranging from beautiful magnolias and lilacs which flower in the spring to hydrangea, honeysuckles, and jasmines, which bloom in the summer to Japanese maples which bring gorgeous color in the fall. Evergreens too can add that curb appeal to your property. In this chapter we will talk about the proper care of landscape trees and shrubs. We will cover different deciduous and carnivorous trees which you can have as both trees and bushes in your yard. All these trees and shrubs are well manicured and pruned to maintain shape and style. You will also learn how you can manipulate certain trees and shrubs to train them to grow into a certain shape.

Deciduous Trees and Shrubs

Deciduous trees and shrubs are those trees and shrubs which shed their leaves in the fall and go dormant in the winter. Many fruit trees and decorative flowering trees are deciduous and loose their leaves in the fall, blossom in the spring, grow foliage in early summer. Some decorative deciduous trees for your landscape are listed below.

A. **Magnolias** are a very popular landscape tree, though they can be high maintenance. Also called tulip trees, magnolias are known for their white and purple tulip-like blossoms in mid April to mid May. Magnolias do grow large and constantly need to be pruned to maintain shape. Magnolias also grow sucker shuts which need to be cut off. We'll get into sucker shoots and why they need to be clipped when they're young later.

B. **Japanese maples** are an amazing addition to your landscape. Especially popular as accent pieces in rock and water garden areas. There are many varieties of Japanese maples from the verdis variety, which have emerald green lace like leaves which turn into a coral red color in the fall to small maples with purple lace like leaves to large purple large leaf maples. When young, Japanese maples are often cultivated in Japan for bonsai trees because of their unique shape and manipulatability.

C. **Forsythia** are a wonderful shrub which can look great standing alone as an accent piece or planted next to other forsythia for a hedge. These are often popular for their bright yellow blossoms in early spring and dense foliage in the summer. Forsythia do need to be cut back from time to time in the summer.

D. **Cherry trees** not only provide delicious fruit in the summer, but in late spring they have beautiful white blossoms to decorate your yard. Like magnolias, cherry trees can grow sucker shotes.

E. **Redbud trees** are native to the northern part of the United States. They have become a popular landscape tree for their pinkish purple blossoms in the springtime. Redbuds can grow sucker shotes which need to be kept in check.

F. **Lilacs** are wonderful green shrubs which offer fragrant white, purple or dark purple flowering plumes in late May or early June.

G. **Jasmines** offer dark green foliage all summer long and small white fragrant blossoms in early to mid June.

H. **Honeysuckles** are actually a vine, not a tree nor shrub, but when properly trained to grow on a trellis or pergola, they can take on tree-like characteristics. They are fast growers and blossom during the summer months. Because they are prolithic growers, they need to cut back several times during the summer.

I. **Trumpet vines** are also vines, but grow much larger than honeysuckles. They are given their name because of large trumpet shaped orange flowers which bloom in late August. Trumpet vines are high maintenance and do seed. They can be invasive, so they need to be kept in check.

J. **Boxwoods** are one of the few evergreen varieties of deciduous shrubs. Boxwoods are wonderful trees which can also be manipulated to grow as bushes. They have a small leaf, but it grows densely, making it an ideal hedge tree.

K. **Dogwoods** offer beautiful foliage with small red inedible berries during the summer, but during May, they have amazing white blossoms which bloom for over a month before growing leaves.

L. Hibiscus come in different varieties. Not all hibiscus do well in colder climates, so some may need to be potted plants and brought in for the winter. One popular hibiscus tree for colder areas is the rose of Sharon. These bloom with purple flowers in August and September. Rose of Sharon hibiscus can be very invasive as they do seed profusely in the winter, so they do need to be kept in check. You may want to remove the seed pods as they begin to mature and loose their green color.

M. Bittersweet is a wood-stem vine and has thick dense foliage in the summertime but during the winter it produces reddish yellow inedible berries and gives a nice look to your property in the fall. Bittersweet is ideal to train on unsightly chainlink fences to give the look of a hedge. Bittersweet is low maintenance, but because it does grow, it should be cut back a few times in the summer.

The list for deciduous landscape trees and shrubs can go on for a long time, but some of the more popular trees and shrubs are listed above.

What are sucker shotes? Basically, if you look at Figure One below, a sucker shote is a small shote which begins to grow leaves which grows separate from the trunk of the original tree. Sucker shotes are not branches. They grow from the crown of the tree and need to be clipped at the base. The problem with sucker shotes is they suck out all the energy and nutrients the tree needs from its root system. This in effect starves the main trunk of the tree, which will eventually cause it to die. Then the sucker shotes will grow around it and you have this unsightly rotting dead tree trunk in the middle of the mess. As the main trunk dies and begins to rot, then bugs get into it and this can actually cause the crown and the roots to rot, killing the entire tree.

These sucker shotes can grow on many deciduous trees, especially flowering trees, thus extra attention should be paid to your prize flowering trees. Watch around the crown at the base of the trunk by the ground. If you see a new shote grow with leaves on it coming out of your tree's crown or growing out of the ground within inches from your tree, take your pruners and cut it off while it's still young. This can minimize the damage it can cause to your tree in the future.

Figure One: A sucker shote growing out of the root crown of a landscape tree

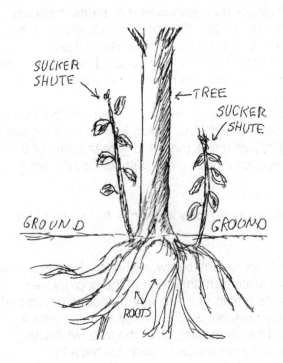

SUCKER
SHUTE

←TREE

SUCKER
SHUTE

GROUND

GROUND

ROOTS

Carnivorous Trees and Shrubs

Carnivorous trees and shrubs are most of your evergreens. In this species of trees and shrubs you find all the needle trees, such as pines, firs, yus, and cedars. Some of the most popular carboniferous landscape trees are listed below.

A. **Blue spruces** are your typical "Christmas tree" evergreens. They are called blue spruce because they are tall fir trees which have a light blue hue on their needles. These grow very tall and large. They begin to produce pinecones in late summer or early fall and have the traditional Christmas tree shape. These are wonderful trees which add beauty all year round and you can also use them Christmas time by lighting them up with Christmas lights. They are very hardy and handle cold weather very well. If you are looking to plant several blue spruces together, be sure you do not plant them closer than ten feet between them. These trees grow big and need the room.

B. **White pines** are your typical long soft needle pine trees and these can be high maintenance. Care for the trees is minimal, but cleaning up after them is where the maintenance comes into play. As they continue to grow new needles year round, they will shed their old ones. If you have a lawn in the shadow of these pines, you will have to clean the needles off the grass, as they will make the soil too acidic for your lawn, killing the grass near the tree. In general white pines can grow bigger and taller than the blue spruce. Keep this in mind when planting more than one of them.

C. **Scotch pines** can be an interesting addition to your landscape. These pines can either grow into a Christmas tree shape or be a rugged gnarled sparse branch. Typically, scotch pines have medium length hard and prickly needles which are a rich green color. The usually produce their pine cones in late summer.

D. **Japanese yus** are often perceived to be a bush or shrub, but it's actually a tree. This is an amazing tree for your landscaping. Japanese yus have short but soft dark green needles and can be manipulated as either bushes or trees by how they are cut and trimmed. When left in it's natural state, the yu will take a bonsai like shape and can grow as tall as 20 feet. If constantly topped from late sapling stage to maturity, it will maintain a specific height and shape. This makes them ideal for evergreen hedges and allows them to be shaped in different shapes as single specimens in your garden.
E. **Cedars** come in different hybrids and they are carnivorous, but do not have needles. They instead have a lace like hard leaf with the hardness of a hard pine needle. Some can have drooping branches where others can grow tall and slender. Ideal for Mediterranean or Middle Eastern themed landscaping.

There are many other trees of the carnivorous family. You need to go to your local nursery to see which evergreen is right for you.

Hydrangea and How you Can Manipulate the Color of their Flowers
Hydrangea are an amazing shrub in the deciduous family. Hydrangea are large bushes which have large leaves in the summertime and depending on the Ph of the soil they grow in, their flowers can be either blue or pink to red. Typically, if the soil is acid, your hydrangea will have flowers which are a pink to red color. The more acidic you make the soil, the more red your hydrangea's flowers become, the more alkaline the soil, the more blue they become. Different hydrangea include oak leaf hydrangea which have leaves that look like large oak leaves and have large ball flowers. Other hydrangea have super large ball flowers, and others yet plume like flowers.

Trees and shrubs add beauty to your landscaping. You also need to keep in mind that some more dense shrubs can also trap dead leaves which are difficult to clean out in the fall. You want to check with your local nursery to find out which trees and shrubs are right for you. Of course, you might want to check the USDA climate zone map, however, most nurseries in your area will carry only trees which can handle the climate in the USDA zone where you live in.

Chapter Three

Choosing and Controlling Ground Cover

What is ground cover? Basically, ground cover is a vine-like plant which grows and spreads on the ground. It is a leafy and sometimes flowering vine or runner plant which densely covers dirt and is ideal for areas where you cannot have lawn or flowerbeds. Ground covers are generally low maintenance, however, many varieties of ground cover are fast growers and do need to be kept back to keep them from taking over your whole landscaping. Some ground covers can also be trained to grow up walls to add that special look. In this chapter, you will learn the following:

A. Different common varieties of ground cover, how they grow, how invasive they are and how and when to plant them.
B. Where to use ground cover in your landscaping project.
C. Keeping ground cover under control, by using edging, trimming, and cutting back.
D. Maintenance for your ground cover.

Different Varieties of Ground cover
There are many varieties of ground cover, some of which have some beautiful flowers in the spring, but all have nice foliage to cover unsightly ground in your yard.   Though there are many different varieties of ground covers out their, this chapter will give you the most common varieties which are sold at most nusreries and garden centers.

A. Myrtle is a common ground cover which is very low maintenance. Myrtle is ideal for those who live in forested areas which many oaks, maples, and large pine trees. Myrtle loves acidic soil and thrives in the American midwest and the Great Lakes regions due to the high acidity in the soil. Myrtle will spread quickly, so there is some maintenance and we recommend you have edging at the edge of the area where you have your myrtle growing. In the springtime, myrtle has a purple bluish like violet shaped flower. Myrtle will trap leaves in the fall, but don't get bent out of shape if some of the leaves stay trapped in the myrtle. Myrtle will decompose these leaves and you will not see them in the spring after your yard cleanup.

B. Pachysandra is a ground cover which grows in the same environment and USDA climate zone as myrtle. The difference is that pachysandra will grow where there is more sun, but will also grow in the shade. Pachysandra grows a little taller than myrtle and its leaves are larger and have a lighter green color. Pachysandra is not as invasive as myrtle and takes longer to get established when planted. The best time to plant pachysandra is during the early springtime before it flowers. Pachysandra has a white small flower which blooms from early April to mid May.

C. Ivy is more a vine than ground cover, however, it can be used as ground cover. Ivy is very easy to propagate. Simply clip a piece off and put it in a glass of water until it grows roots, then plant. The best time to plant ivy outside is in the early spring and it will need a lot of water to establish itself. Ivy can also be used to grow on walls as well as ground cover to give that look of antiquity and sense of abandonment if that is your theme. One caveat with ivy, however, is that it can damage the mortaring in masonry when it grows on masonry walls. Likewise, it can cause rot on wooden structures, so keep it under control when you allow it to grow on walls.

D. Yewanimus is also an interesting ground cover which has similar properties as ivy, but can grow into tree-like clumps in certain areas. Like ivy, yewanimus can be invasive, so be prepared for high maintenance to keep it under control when planting it. Yewanimus can have small solid light green to green and yellow variegated oval leaves and can give an interesting look to parts of your yard. One problem you might encounter with Yewanimus is it can be a big leaf trap in the fall and can be difficult to clean all the leaves out. Yewanimus can handle both shade and sun and requires little watering.

E. **Foam flower** is a nice ground cover which grows very well in the more colder climates in the US and Canada. Foam flower is a more lighter ground cover and does need ample watering in the summertime. Foam flower likes more shady areas and has small white, pink, or light blue flowers in late spring to early summer.

There are many other varieties of different ground covers available. You will want to look at what zone you are located in on the USDA climate zone map or contact your local nursery or garden center to find out which ground cover is the best for you.

Where to Use Ground cover

Ground cover can be planted for a variety of reasons. If you have areas in your yard which are too shady for flowering plants and weeds tend to dominate the area, thicker ground covers, such as myrtle or pachysandra can add beauty to those areas and keep the weeds to a minimum. Most weeds cannot compete with ground cover for nutrients in the soil and will simply die off. Furthermore, thicker ground covers, such as myrtle, pachysandra, ivy, or yewanimus will give a thick green leafy blanket which can prevent most weeds from growing up.

For those of you who live in sandy areas, like parts of the southern Lake Michigan shoreline in northern Illinois and Indiana and southwestern Michigan, sandy dunes with little or no trees can be a real mess when you have a torrential rain. These above mentioned ground covers do have a thick root system which can hold those sandy dunes together and prevent erosion. Ground cover also looks very good along the edges of your lawn with stone edging dividing the ground cover from the grass.

Keeping Ground Cover Under Control

As mentioned above, many varieties of ground cover can be very invasive. In some cases it has to be to do its job in the yard. Invasive vines and runner plants tend to keep the weeds at bay, but if not controlled, they can take over your landscaping and you can have a huge mess.

Edging is the ideal way to contain your ground cover. Edging can be done in a wide variety of ways, however, you want your edging to go at least three or four inches in the ground with an inch above the ground. This is to limit the spread of runners for ground covers like myrtle, pachysandra, or foam flower. Vine-like ground covers, like ivy and yewanimus can grow over edging, so it is not a good idea to use those in areas which border your lawns. Different types of edging you can use are listed below.

A. **Plastic edging** is cheap and if done right, it is barely visible. Plastic edging is sold in large coils and can be found in many big box stores, like Walmart, Lowe's, or Home Depot for a relatively low price, thus ideal for the landscape design on a budget. The problem with plastic edging, however, is that it can be very difficult to manipulate when you uncoil it. The trick with plastic edging is to put it out on concrete in the sun when you unwrap it. Because the plastic edging is black, it will absorb the heat from the sun rather quickly and will soften itself, making it more pliable. First, you want to place the unwrapped coils with all the ties cut on your hot asphalt or concrete driveway in the hot summer sun and let it heat up for an hour or so. Then proceed to slowly uncoil it. It is a gradual process, but after about two hours in a hot summer day, the plastic edging will loose its curves and you can pretty much bend it how you want. Because the plastic is black, it will stay hot for a while, at least long enough for you to place it in the area where you want to make your border. Use some heavy duty galvanized landscaping spikes to fasten your edging in place. When the plastic edging is hot, it can be easily penetrated with those spikes also.

B. **Wooden timbers or railroad ties** have been a standard for borders in American yards for a long time. If you do use wood timbers, you want to make sure that it is pressure treated lumber, as it will rot much slower than untreated wood. Many garden centers will have railroad ties which they get from the railroads when they replace them. They are cheap as they are of no more use to the railroads. These are heavily treated with petroleum and tar, so they will last more than 20 years before they begin to rot. Use heavy duty galvanized spikes to fasten them on top of each other. You might want to drill holes before driving the spikes in. These spikes should be at least one-eighth of an inch in diameter and seven inches long as a minimum. Position the wooden timbers or railroad ties in a brick-like fashion for extra strength.

C. **Decorative concrete slab** is another common form of edging. Many of the big home improvement stores, like Lowe's or Home Depot carry concrete slabs with scalloped tops for edging and they are also relatively cheap. You can also find these edging slabs at places which sell pavers and other concrete products, such as cinder blocks. Concrete slab edging is fairly easy to install. Simply dig a small trench for the depth of half the slab and place each slab next to each other.

D. **Natural stone** also makes for good edging material. Different types of stones which can be used include slabs of flagstone, which is flat stone, or fieldstone boulders. Most home improvement stores, like Lowe's or Home Depot can be limited in the extent of natural stone, if they carry it at all, so you might want to go to a stone yard or landscape specialty place to find the stone of choice. Stone yards can be a great source, as they can have all kinds of different stone in a variety of colors from different parts of the US and Canada. Placing the stone edging is simple enough. Make a trench and simply hammer the flagstone slabs in with a rubber mallet. Fieldstone can be placed next to each other and sometimes, you may want to mortar them together (See Chapter Six) to give a small wall effect. Different varieties of flagstone sold at most landscaping places and stone yards are listed below.

4. **Pennsylvania blue stone** is a variety of shale and has a bluish grayish color. Sometimes it may have a slight green hue to it as well. Works wonderful as edging stone.

5. **White limestone** is a common variety of flagstone which can sometimes have fossils in it. Limestone is quarried in many parts of the United States, so it is readily available.

6. **Quartzite** is a metamorphic form of granite. This has a shiny sparkle to it because of all the silica and small quartz formations in it.

7. **Colorado red stone** is actually sandstone and has a red color to it. Will compliment the green of most ground covers beautifully.

8. **Slate** can have a grayish black or slight grayish red color to it and can look very beautiful as an edge.

E. **Metal edging** can be very difficult to install, but it is available. Metal edging is also very expensive and can only be found in specialty landscaping shops. If you like metal edging, we recommend you hire a professional to install it, as it can look ugly if not installed properly.

Maintenance

Typically, ground cover is very low maintenance when it comes to fertilizing and care. Most ground covers can store moisture, so they may only need watering when it is very dry. Lighter ground covers, such as foam flower do require watering, but the need to weed is very low, as most ground covers make it impossible for weeds to grow and take over. Basic maintenance for most ground covers is to cut it back when you notice it creeping over your borders. Ivy and yewanimus in particular can be high maintenance when established, as they will frequently need to be cut back since they can spread rather quickly.

Ground cover is easily planted and will establish itself by the end of the summer and thrive if you plant it in early spring. Though not recommended, if you have to plant or transplant ground cover in the summertime, you should water it profusely.

Chapter Four

Proper Lawn Maintenance in the Summer and Fall

The lawn is the biggest pride and joy for most Americans. The tradition of having that beautiful green lawn actually came from England, where lawns were planted as field space between flowerbeds and manicured bushes in the formal garden. Most Americans embrace the more British style lawn with no dandelions or other field flowers in it, unlike Europeans who enjoy having the monotonous green lawn be speckled with the yellow flowers of the dandelions in the summer. Whatever your style, you will learn the basics of lawn maintenance here.

Maintaining your Lawn Mower and other Lawn Equipment
Before you can even start thinking about having that nice green manicured lawn which is evenly cut, you need to think about having a good quality lawnmower which is properly maintained. Knowing the different types of lawnmowers out on the market is also key. Mowing the lawn can either be a relaxing summer activity for some, or for others a long and laborious task. Lawns are high maintenance, so having the right mower for the right lawn is key to ensure you can enjoy a beautiful green lawn all summer long. Some of the different types of mowers are listed below.

A. **Two-cycle engine gas mower** is a regular push mower which has a two-cycle engine. This type of lawnmower is typically an older machine and requires oil be mixed with the gas to run it, as it does not take oil separately with a filter. You need to make sure you mix your gasoline with two-cycle engine oil to the proper instruction specifications, otherwise the fuel will burn too hot and that can cause the engine to burn out. This type of mower is a push mower, which means you have to walk behind it and push it to mow the lawn. If you have a large lawn, it can take a whole day to mow the lawn.
B. **Four-cycle engine gas mower** is also a push mower, like the one mentioned above. A four cycle engine is easier to operate than a two-cycle engine for a lawn mower. Most lawnmowers you buy today have four-cycle engines. All riding mowers are four-cycle engines. A four-cycle engine is a smaller version of the engine in your car. You fuel it up with straight gas and no oil. You do need oil, but it gets put in a separate tank and is used to lubricate the pistons of the engine. Most push mowers are small and are great for smaller lawns, but because you have to walk behind them and push them, they can take for ever with bigger lawns.
C. **Electric mowers** are great for the environmental conscious, but they can be a pain. Electric mowers do not run on a battery and unless you have a small yard with a relatively small

lawn, they are worthless. The biggest problem with electric mowers is that you need a long extension cord and you need to be careful not to cut the cord when you are mowing the lawn.

D. Riding mowers are lawnmowers on which you can ride on and they typically have two or three rotating blades under the mowing deck. These are ideal for people who have acreage and large lawns. Some riding mowers can be like small tractors where others are simply a seat on top of a mowing deck with wheels and a steering wheel and an exhaust pipe that can bag the clippings.

E. Garden or lawn tractors are wonderful machines to have. Not only do they have a mowing deck, but they can also perform other maintenance functions, such as leaf removal and some are even equipped with a small snowplow to plow your driveway in the wintertime.

Smaller lawn maintenance equipment is also needed to take care of the edges to make your lawn clean and even during the summer and to remove the leaves in the fall. Most of these tools run on two-cycle engines, however, in the spring, you will also need a special thatching rake. Regular maintenance tools other than a lawnmower are listed below.

A. Thatching rakes are mostly a manual tool. There are some thatching rakes which run on a two-cycle engine, but thatching your lawn in early spring is best done by hand. It is a difficult job to do, but it needs to be done. Thatching gets rid of all the dead grass accumulated over the previous year. Getting rid of the thatch will make your lawn breathe better and make it more robust and much greener. A typical thatching rake has wire tines which are thin and can dig into the soil base of the lawn and bring up the dead thatch, which you can then bag and throw into your compost heap.

B. Weedwackers are a small machine with a motor head equipped with a two-cycle engine. Under the motor head, there is a long drive shaft which has a rotor attached to the bottom of it. Typically, weedwackers use a thick heavy plastic string which works like a whip and knocks down the taller blades of grass in areas where the lawnmower cannot get to. You need the weedwacker to bring down the grass along the edges of your lawn, next to flowerbeds, along your house, patios, or other landscape features in your yard.

C. Edgers are used to cut parts of the lawn which encroach onto concrete areas of your yard, such as driveways, walks, or patios. The edger is of a similar structure as a weedwacker and run on a two-cycle engine. The edger has a thick metal blade which will dig into the sod at the edge of the concrete area in your yard. You can also successfully edge your lawn with a flat spade by jabbing it down vertically at the edge of the concrete. You then remove the excess lawn and you have beautiful clean cut edges separating your lawn from your driveway, patio, or walk.

D. Spreader which can evenly spread fertilizer. Fertilizing your lawn is important so you do need a spreader. You want to get a good quality spreader which can adjust the amount it can spread because too little fertilizer can keep your lawn from staying green all summer, and too much chemical fertilizer, like Scotts or other like brands can burn your lawn and make it turn yellow.

E. Leaf blowers are important for the fall. Dead leaves are your lawn's worst enemy. If they are allowed to accumulate on your lawn, they can cause the soil to become acidic and allow for moss spores to take over, killing the grass. Typically, leaves need to be removed in the fall twice and once in the spring. There are two types of leaf blowers you can use. You can also rake the leaves by hand, but that's tedious.

    9. Backpack and hand blowers run on two-cycle engines and can be carried on your back or in your hand. They have a high power fan which channels forced air through a large tube and blows the leaves from the front.

10. **Push blowers** are ideal for larger lawns. Push blowers run on four-cycle engines and need to have the oil changed periodically, like your lawnmower. They have a jet turbine fan and the best ones have an airflow divider. The airflow divider is great because it allows air to get under the leaves to lift them up and the other half of the airflow to move the leaves forward.

F. **Spike roller** might be needed in certain soil conditions. This makes small holes in the soil bed of your lawn which can allow for the grass roots of your lawn to breathe and get the oxygen they need.

Proper maintenance for your lawnmower is key. Unless you are good at mechanics, you should take your lawnmower to a small engines shop to have maintenance work on it. Avoid big box stores, such as Lowe's or Home Depot to fix and maintain your machines. They usually send them away to a centralized location and you can be without your mower for a long time. Local small engine shops are the best and their reputations are easy to find out. Go to one with a good reputation and work will usually be done in one or two days, unless a part needs to be ordered. Below are DIY maintenance and shop maintenance.

A. **Changing oil** can be done either by yourself or at a shop. If you're in doubt, take it to the shop. If the oil is not properly changed, your lawnmower will not run properly and you can get an uneven cut when you mow the lawn. Every time you change the oil, you need to change the oil filter also.

B. **Changing the air filter** may need to be done periodically. Pollens and dust can restrict the airflow to the engine and that can keep your mower from starting properly. You can do this your self if you are familiar with engines, otherwise take it to the shop.

C. **Sharpening rotoblades** should be done at the shop. They have the right tools to do the job and having sharp blades ensures a nice evenly cut lawn.

What brands of machines are good quality? Well, in our business, we obviously used professional grade equipment. We do not recommend purchasing machinery at big box stores. These stores, like Lowe's or Home Depot are fine for purchasing some inexpensive items and hardware for your landscaping project, but the machines they sell are usually of a lower quality and parts tend to need to be replaced more frequently. Most big box stores will carry brands, like MTD or Yard Man. These may be Ok if you have a small lawn and live in a dry area, such as the Southwest where mowing is not that frequent.

In more moist and temperate climates, you want to get brands which are known for quality and are durable. You are better off finding these machines at a local garden center. Furthermore, these garden centers also have a machine shop and many of them are licensed dealers for a particular line of mowers and other gas power tools. Some of the best machines for your landscaping are listed below.

A. **Toro** is a very well known brand and many garden or landscape shops which sell machinery are licensed to sell Toro equipment. Toro primarily makes lawn mowers, including Lawnboy. Toro also makes the Wheelhorse line of rider mowers and garden tractors. These are also good machines. Most Toro machines have a Briggs & Stratton four cycle engine and a licensed dealer will have the knowledge on all the products made by this brand. In fact, many professional landscapers use Toro mowers and most of their small push mowers are Lawnboys, simply because of the reputation of this brand. Most Toro machinery is also made in the United States.

B. **Echo** is a Japanese brand which makes two-cycle engine blowers and power tools for the yard. In our business we always used Echo, because the quality was of a high standard and the machines required very little maintenance. Echo has a line of powerful backpack blowers which can get leaves moving, even when they are somewhat wet. Echo also has a line of weedwackers, edgers, power clippers, and more.

C. **Stihl** is a German brand which, like Echo makes a line of high quality line of two-cycle engine power tools. Stihl makes machines similar to Echo and the quality is the same as Echo. Many professional landscapers do use Stihl machines.

D. **Husqvarna** are best known for their chainsaws, but they also have a small line of two-cycle engine tools for landscaping. Husqvarna is a Swedish brand and their machines are of a superior quality, especially their flagship product line of chainsaws. Husqvarna may not have a variety of lawn care power tools, but they do make weedwackers and edgers.

Mixing oil and gasoline for your two-cycle engines can be a challenge. Some of the old-timers might tell you that you can mix old car oil with the gas for your two-cycle engines, but that's no longer true, especially if they are machinery made by Echo, Stihl, or Husqvarna. These brands do have high quality engines and their engine oil has special additives which are needed in the oil-fuel mix. If you use a lesser quality oil for these machines, the gas could burn too hot and burn out the engine. That can get expensive, as it would void the warrantee. Furthermore, be prepared to pay a stiff price for a Toro lawnmower or Echo, Stihl, or Husqvarna power tools. They are high quality, so the price is well worth it.

One other reason to use Echo oil with Echo machines, Stihl oil with Stihl machines, and Husqvarna oil with Husqvarna machines is that different brands may have a different oil-gas mixing ratio. These brands will also make the oil with a pre-measured cup which can give you the exact ratio per gallon of gas. Using the recommended oil-gas mix ratio is crucial, as not enough oil in the gasoline can cause it to burn hot, damaging the motor and too much can gum up the carburetor and other moving parts of the motor, making it difficult to start.

Fertilizing your Lawn

Here is where most lawns can be a success and have a lush green carpet for your yard, or can be a nasty unsightly yellow mess of dead grass. Proper fertilization is critical for a good lawn. There are two different types of fertilizers available for your lawn, chemical and organic. These two will be covered below.

Chemical fertilizer is fertilizer which is of a chemical base. All fertilizers are made from treated sewage or poultry excrement. The problem is that treated sewage is more common with most chemical fertilizers, as it is cheap. Furthermore, most chemical fertilizers and lawn treatment companies, such as Scotts and TruGreen, contain special chemicals which selectively kill weeds, like dandelions and crabgrass, which often can affect the look of your lawn. TruGreen is typically a franchise which has a contract which you can hire to fertilize your lawn for you. Scotts also has a service, but they can also sell you the actual fertilizer with instructions on how to apply it. If you are too concerned that you might fertilize your lawn the wrong way and apply too much or too little fertilizer, you might want to leave it to a professional to do it for you. This is because fertilizers used by TruGreen and Scotts are harsh chemical agents and can burn your lawn if not applied properly. A burnt lawn causes those large areas of dead yellow grass where too much fertilizer was applied. Use chemical fertilizer with caution.

Organic fertilizer is by far the better route. Not only can chemical fertilizer be harsh on your lawn, but once applied, you, your children and pets cannot go on the lawn for a couple of days after the fertilizer was applied, due to harsh reactions it can cause to skin. With organic fertilizer, you don't have this problem.

The great thing about organic fertilizers is that they are natural. Many companies who produce organic fertilizers will research each plant and develop the right fertilizer with natural ingredients to give your lawn that beautiful lush green look. Most organic fertilizers are baked manure pellets which then dissolve into the soil once wet, thus it is natural and full of the nitrogen rich nutrients your lawn needs without being harmful to your children or pets.

Winterization

Winterizing your lawn is basically preparing it for winter. Like many other plants in temperate and cold climates, your lawn will go dormant during the late fall into winter. You will notice the grass will loose its bright emerald green color and be more dull. This is normal. Like in the springtime, you should rake your lawn and remove thatch from your lawn, especially if you mulch when you mow. This can make it easier on your grass and can reduce the risk of added decaying plant matter, which can cause moss spores to set in.

Give your lawn a good spreading of lime when the trees are in fall color and before the leaves begin to fall. The lime will ensure the soil in which the grass grows will maintain the proper Ph level.

Remove leaves when you see a blanket of them on your lawn. Preferably remove the leaves before it rains. When dead leaves get wet in the fall, they dry very slowly, and become more difficult to remove.

Moles and Other Lawn Pests

The biggest problem for lawns are those pesky moles. Moles are like mice, once you see one, there are a thousand more. This problem is very simple to solve. Moles want the grubs. Kill the grubs, the moles go away. See what your garden center can do.

road-packChapter Five

Paving and Creating Paths

What is paving? Well, paving can mean a wide variety of things, such as paving your driveway or a road with asphalt, but this is not really the kind of paving we have in mind here. Here paving is done with paver bricks or cobble stones. You will also learn how to make a cobble stone driveway, patio, or walkways. You can also mix your own concrete and add color to it, some of this will be covered in this chapter, but concrete and masonry will be covered in more detail in Chapter Six. You will also learn about using road-pack, pea gravel and river rock for paths and natural driveways. There are so many things you can do with paving stones, flagstone, and other stones to make your yard a landscape that looks like a million dollars.

In this chapter, you will learn the basics for making paths, walks, patios, and driveways which will last a long time. You will learn the basics of mixing and pouring concrete and how to compose your landscape design and how to make walks and paths which will match your landscape theme. The basic steps in this chapter include:

A. **The basic materials** needed for paving. What is packing sand and moon dust. You will also learn about why using packing sand or even better moon dust as a packing medium for your pavers. Road pack is also crucial, especially for driveways and other areas for your yard.
B. **Paver bricks and cobblestones** and how to install them to make them level and what tools you will need to keep these pavers and cobblestones in place and tightly.
C. **Use of packing material** to create a solid bed for paver or cobblestone walks, patios, and driveways.
D. **Mixing and pouring concrete** and how to pour concrete and spread it properly for driveways or walkways. Mixing your concrete yourself versus having a truck pour it for you. The basic tools needed for spreading and leveling concrete.
E. **Use of road-pack** and how to apply it as a basic bed for a gravel driveway or broad path.
F. **Decorative gravel,** such as river rock, pea gravel, or large pebbles.
G. **Making flagstone paths** to go across your lawn or maintenance paths in your flowerbeds. Flagstone paths can also be created to make those natural and rustic walks through large garden areas in your landscaping.

The Basic Materials for Paving
Before choosing your design for walks, patios, or driveways, you will need to know how to prepare your paved areas before paving. You will have to create an outer structure for your paved area. The basics will be covered below.

Building your outline is key to building your patio, driveway, or walks. When building your driveway can be a bit more challenging as it will have to be created with extra packing material under the pavers to support the weight of the cars which will be using the driveway. Outlines can be built with a variety of materials depending on your personal tastes. Some of the common outline materials used for walks or patios are mentioned below.

A. **Pressure treated timbers** are commonly used together with paver bricks, cobblestones, or other paver blocks. The nice thing about pressure treated timbers is that you can use them as gridding to add division and sectioned patterns on your walks or paths.
B. **Metal edging** is another idea for creating a more modern look to your walks or patios.
C. **Interlocking blocks** are commonly used. One well known brand, Unilock, is the biggest manufacturer of interlocking blocks and paver bricks. Unilock products are primarily made from molded concrete and can be found at many landscaping stores, home improvement stores, or warehouse stores, such as Lowe's or Home Depot. Unilock products are great for people who do not have experience paving, as they interlock very simple to install.

D. **Stone sectioning** can be used as an outline for more rustic walks using cobblestones. Some common stone sectioning include large long slabs of flagstone, fieldstone, or other specialty stone.

If you look at Figure One below, you can see how the outline of your paved area needs to be built. When it comes to your outline, it will have to be set up to hold at least six inches of depth plus the depth of the pavers you are using. You may want to put more packing medium than the intended level for your pavers. This will ensure that the pavers when tamped down, the packing material will come down to level. This is especially true with packing sand.

Figure One: Building your outline

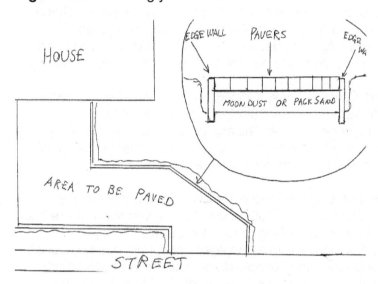

Notice how this form made from pressure treated timbers is built with the depth in mind for the packing material.

Packing material is critical for making a level paved area. When working with pavers, you need to understand that any soft area can cause your paved area to sink and it will no longer level. The most common packing materials are listed below.

Packing sand is basically mason sand, which is quarried from riverbeds. The reason why packing or mason sand is from riverbeds is because the the grains are finer, thus the sand packs better and becomes much harder than the coarser sand grains found in beach or lake bed sand, which tends to have a softer packing quality. This kind of sand will not allow for a tight and hard bed needed for paver bricks or cobblestones.

The drawbacks of packing sand is that sand is sand. It can erode if you have water flow underneath your paved area, it can erode and your pavers could sink and you may have to reinstall your pavers.

Moon dust is the packing material of choice for many landscapers. When we had our business, we only used moon dust as a packing material. More expensive than packing sand, moon dust makes a more solid bed, as it is finely crushed limestone. It is white in color, like something on the moon's surface, hence its name. Moon dust not only packs well, but when it gets wet, it will get hard and will make a stable bed which will keep your pavers level.

Road pack is a mixture of crushed limestone and limestone gravel. Road pack is primarily used as a basic road bed as it does pack down into a solid base. A mix of road pack and moon dust is an ideal bed for your driveway, as the two materials combined together will support the weight of a car or pickup truck.

Paver Bricks and Cobblestones

Paver bricks and cobblestones can add some amazing features to your yard. There is a large variety of paver bricks, some of which are made from molded concrete, clay, or stone. Stone pavers can be fairly expensive and depending on the kind of stone, the cost can go up. Concrete pavers are more inexpensive and large brands, such as Unilock can give you a wide variety of styles and colors. The problem with concrete pavers, you do compromise on quality.

The most common clay brick paver is the Chicago brick. Chicago bricks are old bricks and are not made anymore. Basically, in the late 19th and early 20th Centuries, there was a manufacturer of bricks located in Chicago, known as the Chicago Brick Company. This manufacturer made most of the paver bricks which were used to pave the streets in many US towns. Though Chicago bricks are not made anymore, they are readily available.

How and where do I find Chicago bricks? Chicago bricks are found in many old towns throughout the US. You need to contact the municipal authorities of any given town where brick streets are common or who's street department is looking to redo the streets. Many municipalities have paved over the old brick streets with a thin layer of asphalt, but the asphalt has come off, exposing the brick. Furthermore, many people do not like the old brick streets because of the noise when cars go over it, so many of the Chicago bricks are torn out and streets are repaved using modern technology. Many cities and towns who remove street paver bricks will either sell them at a discounted price or give them away.

The biggest problem when using old Chicago bricks is that you might not have enough pavers to pave a large area. For this reason, we recommend that you use Chicago bricks as accents and mix them with cobblestones to make a real statement.

You do need to take into account that the Chicago Brick Company, which manufactured the Chicago bricks has been out of business for over 60 years, so as more people gather those bricks for accent pieces or the look of antiquity to their projects, they can become harder to find as time progresses.

Specialty paver bricks can be found in many landscape shops, some nurseries, brick retailers, or concrete and masonry stores. Stone yards are another good place to look for specialty paver bricks, some of which are made from natural stone.

Besides clay, some specialty paver bricks are made from slate, shale, granite, or limestone. The natural stone bricks can be pricy, but they do look very good on your walks.

Cobblestones are similar to paver bricks, but the difference is that they are shaped differently and are all made from natural stone. Most cobblestones are made from a hard igneous rock, such as granite, quartzite, or metamorphic rock, such as slate or marble. We do not recommend marble for outside, however, as it is a soft stone and does not weather well. Some cobblestones can also be made from your basic sedimentary rock, such as limestone or shale.

Cobblestones tend to have a more square shape versus the rectangular shape of paver bricks. Cobblestones are also smaller, which allows you to position them in a pattern giving a mosaic like character to them and cobblestones are also designed to give that feeling of antiquity, thus they are roughly hone as the cobblestones used to pave roads in ancient times.

Paver tiles can also look very nice, though care should be used when using the tamper when tamping the tile in place, as too much force on a power tamper can crack the tile. Most paver tiles are made from natural stone and the variety is amazing. You can also get some paver tiles in terra cotta clay for that Mediterranean or southwest affect. Stone tile is typically made from a variety of stone, which includes granite, quartzite, shale, slate, lannon, alabaster, sandstone, or limestone. Some paver tile made from sandstone, shale, or limestone have fossils in them giving all that more interesting of a look to your patio. Paver tiles should not be used for driveways, because the weight of the car can crack them over time. See Figures Two through Four to see different patterns you can do with paver bricks, cobblestones, and tiles.

Figure Two: Paver bricks in a herringbone fashion

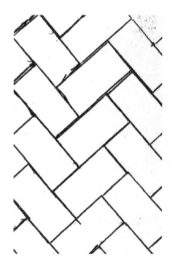

Figure Three: Paver bricks in square and traditional brick fashion

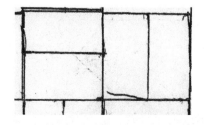
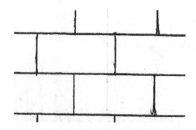

Square Fashion

Traditional Brick Fashion

Figure Four: Cobblestone patterns

Use of Packing Material

What is packing material? Well, as mentioned above, mason sand, moon dust, and road pack are all different packing materials used to create a solid bed for pavers. Our suggestion is that you use moon dust as the bed for pavers. Once you place the moon dust down on the bed, you want to make sure you grade it across and check it with a level to see if it is level. You want several inches of moon dust to make sure the pavers have a solid enough bed to sit on. After you set the pavers in the desired position, you will want to throw a layer of mason sand on top of the pavers. Put about an inch of mason sand on top of the pavers and make sure the sand covers the pavers. Run the power tamper on the pavers. The sand will protect the pavers from the impact of the power tamper and some of the mason sand will also fall in the cracks between the pavers, filling them and giving that extra pressure holding the pavers tightly and pushing them outward towards the frame you created. (See Figure One above)

Once the pavers are tamped in and are solid enough for you to walk on them without moving, then take a hose with a high-powered water jet nozzle to wash off the excess sand from the top of the bricks. You can then use the level to check if the pavers are level.

Making a driveway requires a stronger bed, so you should first place a hefty layer of road pack for a good seven inches and moon dust for a good four inches on top of that. Then place the pavers on top and do the process described in the above paragraph.

Mixing and Pouring Concrete

Concrete is another way you can create a solid driveway or walks around your home. You can also get some molds which you can use to add texture to the concrete surface to give that cobblestone look, brick, or natural stone look. You can also add extra pea gravel to the mix and hose the concrete to give that speckle stone look to your concrete walks or driveway.

The difference between concrete and mortar is like night and day. Mortar is more like a glue to hold brick or stone together. It is more solid (See Chapter Six), whereas concrete is more liquid when poured.

Mixing concrete can be difficult and very labor intensive if you have a large area to pour. If you have a driveway to pour, then you may want to have a cement truck come and pour the driveway. Cement trucks do have a large mixing cylinder which can hold two or three tons of concrete and mix it on the road. This will make the job go faster, however, if you have a small sitting area to pour and want to do it yourself, you can rent a gas or electric concrete mixer from your local general rental place. This is like a miniature cement truck and can mix two to three yards of concrete at a time.

Materials needed for mixing concrete are listed in detail below. It is very important to follow these instructions below, as if one of the steps is done wrong, you can have a weak mix, which can then crack later on or even when it cures.

A. **Get several 80 pound bags of Type I pure Portland cement mix** and use it sparingly. You will learn the different cement mix strength codes in Chapter Six when learning the basics of masonry, but for now, you need to understand that Portland cement is not really a brand of cement. Portland is an ingredient in most cement mixes which adds the strength and hardness to your concrete or mortar. The more Portland in a mix, the stronger and harder it will be after a full cure. Most mortars will not require pure Portland cement (See Chapter 6), but when it comes to mixing concrete, you want pure Portland cement, as it needs to be strong enough to endure all the traffic and punishments from the elements your walks, patios, and driveways endure. You can see whether a cement mix has pure Portland if it has the label "Type I" on the bag. Type I cement mix is pure Portland and made specifically for concrete. Portland cement also absorbs moisture quickly, thus it is ideal for mixing concrete.

B. **Mason sand** is needed to mix with the cement mix. For every shovel of cement mix, you need to add atleast two or three shovels of mason sand. Mason sand serves as a strengthener and also makes the concrete porous, which is necessary. If your concrete cannot breath and allow water vapor to escape, it can cause moisture to freeze in the wintertime, thus cause cracking.

C. **Pea gravel** is needed to add strength to the concrete. Unlike mortar, which is just cement and sand, concrete adds pea gravel to make it stronger. As the concrete sets, the pea gravel will sink to the bottom, so you will not even notice it once it's hard. You want to add at least two shovels of pea gravel to every shovel of sand. For that stone speckle look, you can also add more pea gravel and hose the cement constantly during the setting process to make the pea gravel visible.

Tools needed to mix and pour your own concrete are quite simple. Ideally, we recommend you get a small gas or electric concrete mixer to mix your concrete. This will constantly keep the concrete in motion until you are ready to pour it. Remember, concrete will begin to set if you don't keep it in motion while moving it.

If you cannot get a gas or electric concrete mixer, you should use a large plastic wheel barrel and a mortar hoe. (See Figure Five) A mortar hoe looks like a garden hoe, but has two holes in the blade. The holes are there to allow for the water to flow through it and enhance the mixing of the concrete.

Figure Five: A typical mortar hoe

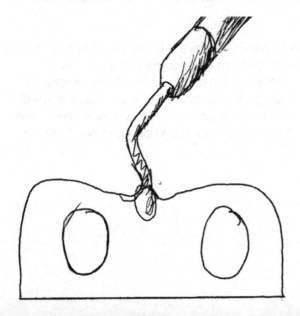

consistency**Adding color to your concrete** is a bit tricky, but it can be done. Do not get the bottles of liquid concrete color sold at home improvement stores, like Lowe's or Home Depot. These are for beginners and it is difficult to get the right consistency with those plus the color is limited.

Many masonry shops will carry color pigments for concrete and mortar. These are powders and usually different oxides of metals and minerals. Any greens or slate colors will contain copper and aluminum oxides. This is because copper oxides are naturally green and aluminum oxides are naturally black. Reds and oranges are primarily iron oxides, and other colors are from different oxides also.

Simply add the powder to the concrete while mixing until you get the desired color. You do want to note that the color will get lighter as the concrete dries and hardens, so the darker you want the color, the more pigment you need to add to your concrete.

Use of Road Pack

When you think of a dirt road or a dirt driveway, that rocky or gravel-like surface is created by road pack. Basically, road pack is coarsely crushed limestone and packs down to become a strong bed of limestone gravel and sand and is often used not only for dirt roads or driveways, but also as a bed for most asphalt roads.

In landscaping, you can use road pack for as a bed for driveways, paths, or walkways. Combine it with moon dust and you have a good bed for adding a thin layer of pea gravel or river rock and pack them down with a power tamper. You then have a nice rustic looking path or driveway.

Decorative Gravel
Decorative gravel is nice gravel which can be used in paths, driveways, or in flowerbeds. Typically, decorative gravel is river rock or crushed specialty rocks, such as shale, volcanic lava rock, and other specimens. The most popular decorative gravel, however, is river rock.

What is river rock? River rock is gravel or small pebbles which have been brought from the bottom or banks of rivers. The stones in river rock are typically rounded or oval in shape and are a mix of granite and limestone. At most landscaping centers, river rock is sold in different sizes and typically are referred by a number, with the exception of pea gravel, which are very small rocks.   The types of river rock and their uses in both landscaping and other uses are listed below.

A. **Pea gravel** is the smallest variety of river rock. As mentioned above, it is a key ingredient in mixing concrete. It can also be used by itself in walks, paths, or open areas for rock gardens. Pea gravel got its name because the pebbles are small enough and are very round to the point that they have the shape and the size of peas. Not the most ideal form of river rock for a drive way, because it can cause traction problems with your car when you try to drive in and out of your driveway. Used lightly over moon dust, you can use some if you pack it down tightly with a power tamper.

B. **Number 8 river rock** has larger pebbles than pea gravel. This type of river rock is good for gravel driveways, however, you should have a good road pack and moon dust bed before you apply the river rock for driveways. Number 8 river rock is also great by itself for open areas in a rock garden, as it does provide good drainage.

C. **Number 5 river rock** are large pebbles and is great for both flower beds, paths, driveways, or large open areas intended for foot traffic. For driveways, you should use a combination of road pack and moon dust to pack it down with a power tamper. Number 5 river rock is excellent for drainage and is also often used in making French drains, which are trenches in areas where rain water often gets trapped and causes low flooding. Having a French drain at the lowest point allows that water to drain quickly and the flooding then ceases to be a problem.

Making Flagstone Paths

Many people like to have flagstone paths to divide their lawns, or to go through the garden areas of their landscaping. Flagstone paths are relatively easy to create and need little or no effort. Some of the more popular varieties of flagstone are listed below.

A. **Colorado or Arizona redstone** is a variety of flat sandstone which is typically quarried in Arizona or Colorado. Some of this type of sandstone can also be quarried in areas of Utah as well. This has a beautiful red color and works well with dark mulches or black dirt. Because red is the complementary color of green, they can also make a statement when you use this type of flagstone with your lawn. When thinking of using Colorado or Arizona redstone, you need to remember that this is sandstone, so it is very soft and can break easily. Consider getting slabs which are several inches thick for path stones.

B. **Shale** is also very common. Often referred to Pennsylvania Blue or Green Stone, because of its color and where it's quarried, it does have a beautiful color. Shale is stronger than sandstone, but can also crack. Like the Colorado or Arizona redstone, it is sold in large slabs and looks very nice as paths in the garden areas.

C. **Limestone** is very common and is your basic flagstone. Limestone can have a variety of color ranging from white to grey to rust color, depending what kind of minerals are in the limestone and where it was quarried. Often, limestone flagstone has fossils in it, giving it interesting character to your garden. Ideal for both lawn and garden paths.

Packing a flagstone path in your lawn does require some work. You want to make sure the slabs of flagstone are flush with the grass, so the lawnmower blades do not hit the stones. The best way to do this is to take a flat blade spade and cut out the sod in the shape of the stone. Fit the stone into the cut out shape and replace any excess sod. Use a hand tamper to lightly tape the stone in until it's snug. It will settle and maintain its place over time as the grass roots regenerate and hold it in place.

Making a flagstone path in your garden areas is very easy. You want to make sure the area where you position your slabs of flagstone is level and that the stones are positioned so they do not shift when people walk on them. Do not place stones on top of mulch, as mulch decays over time and has to be replaced every year. Place the stones first, then apply the mulch.

Everything in this chapter will allow you to have a wonderful landscape with paths, paved areas, and walks to make your yard the envy of the block. Take a look at the style of your house and look at architecture magazines for ideas.

Chapter Six

Enhancing your Landscaping with Stonework

Once you have entered the world of stonework, you bring your landscaping to a whole other level. There are a lot of neat things you can do with stonework and not just features for beauty, bot for both beauty and functionality. In this chapter, you will learn the following:

A. **Learn the basics of stonework.** What is stone work and how can it enhance your landscaping. Learn the different types of stonework which many professional landscapers incorporate in their designs, and how you can create these same things in your own landscaping project.
B. **Dry stacking,** which is the stacking of stone without use of mortar. You will learn the basics of proper dry stacking where stones are securely placed together without being loose and how to use gravity and the weight of the stones to build dry stacked walls, basic fire pits, and other small features.
C. **The basics of masonry.** Learn the difference of mortar, concrete, and grout. you will learn how to mix your own mortar from scratch, the strength codes for cement and mortar mixes to determine the strength of your mortar. You will also learn how to add color to your mortar and create amazing features and make your mortar blend with the stone you are using.
D. **Use of cinder blocks and natural stone** to create your own functional features for your yard. Learn how to build grills, fireplaces, and entertainment areas for outside summer parties.
E. **Fire brick and fire clay,** used to line grills and outdoor fireplaces. What is fire clay, how to use it and make heat proof fire mortar for grills and fireplaces.
F. **Use of boulders** and how they can add special character in your yard.
G. **Building your outdoor sound system** so you can enjoy music in your yard. In this segment, you will also learn how you can build the ultimate entertainment area, such as an outdoor bar with a refrigerator and basic electrical work to make all of it function.

The Basics of Stonework
Stonework is an ancient art which has been used as the basic method of construction by civilizations for millennia. Masonry is also ancient, used by some of the greatest ancient civilizations, such as Rome, Ancient Greece, and a lesser known civilization in the Caucasus, known as Urartu. In the Americas, the ancient Indians, such as the Mayas and the Incas also had advanced methods of stonework to build their civilizations.

There are different types and styles of stonework and you will learn both of them here. Stonework can be used for both landscape features and functional features in your yard. With the use of stone, you can make borders to divide your lawn from flowerbeds, make accent pieces in certain areas of your yard, by placing a boulder or series of boulders to add the illusion of space.

Stonework can also be used for building outdoor kitchens, grills and other things which can make your yard look amazing and have a great place to have summer parties or a good relaxing place to enjoy those wonderful summer afternoons. Basic stone working techniques you will learn in this chapter will be briefly covered below, and in more detail in the following paragraphs.

Dry stacking is the art of stonework without the use of mortar. Dry stacking is a rather difficult method of stone working, but if done right, it will be solid and strong. If done wrong, the stones will be loose and the structure will not hold up strongly or might even fall apart.

Basically, dry stacking should not really be used for building freestanding structures, such as tables or chairs, tables or functional structures. Instead, you can use dry stacking for retaining walls and terraces for flowers.

Masonry is much easier than dry stacking and is not just for stone, but also bricks and cinder blocks. When you know how to work with masonry, the possibilities for enhancing your landscaping are endless. Masonry is a craft, but more importantly, when it involves natural stone, it is an art. Unlike dry stack, masonry uses mortar to glue or bind the stones together. As the mortar dries, it becomes as hard as stone and if mixed properly, it will not even separate from the stones.

Dry stacking

Unless you are a pro at dry stacking, you should keep it limited. Unilock does have special blocks which are specifically designed for dry stacking and this is the easiest way to go for the beginner. What causes the Unilock landscaping concrete blocks stack so easily is because these blocks have a series of grooves and they interlock together, making a strong retaining wall. They are also more inexpensive than natural stone.

If basic concrete blocks like the above mentioned Unilock or other similar brands are too cookie-cutter everybody has them for you, then you can try your hand at dry stacking with natural stone. There are some basic tools you will need when you dry stack with natural stone.

A. **A basic shovel** to dig a base and to sculpt the area where you want to set up your dry stack area.
B. **A flat and broad spade** to detail areas where you may have to dig into the ground and shape the hole for the foundation.
C. **A set of rubber mallets of different sizes** to help pound stones together.

The best stones to use for dry stacking are large and thick slabs of flagstone or flat stones. Though you can dry stack with fieldstone, but because fieldstone which are round and hard to keep together in a dry stack system.

The trick to successfully dry stack flagstone or flat oblong slabs of stone is to take the larger slabs on the bottom and make the smaller stones further up. If you are building a multi-tiered terrace structure on a steep hillside in your backyard or on a steep hilly front yard, you should use some moon dust in parts of the lower terrace to make a stronger base for the upper terraces.

Try not to dry stack a single terrace higher than ten feet unless you really know what you are doing. The reason is that if not done properly, the laws of gravity can prevail and this can cause a dangerous situation.

See Figure One below to show how a dry stacked retaining wall constructed with slabs of flagstone can be properly dry stacked together.

Figure One: Notice the larger stones lower

Note that in some cases, when you build a series of terraces, you may want to use a combination of larger slabs of flagstone which can be used as tie beams. This can be difficult, as long pieces of flagstone, which are strong enough to be used as tie beams, can be hard to find. Furthermore, though flagstone is flat, you should notice that the stones may be uneven. For this reason, you should use a level to make sure your dry stacked wall is level. If necessary, you can take smaller chips of flagstone to add support between the two stones. You can also use moon dust and pebbles to do the same thing.

Figure Two: See how use of moon dust or crushed limestone can be used as a filler between stones

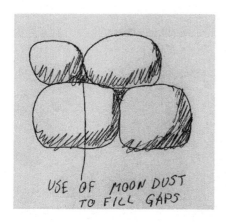

USE OF MOON DUST TO FILL GAPS

different**The Art of Masonry**

What you are about to learn in this section can literally take your landscaping and your backyard into a work of art. You will also learn how to build some amazing features which can let your imagination go wild. Before learning the basics of masonry, you can see in Figures Three to Eight. This is a grill which was built from scratch using masonry with natural stone. Later in this chapter, you will also have a step-by-step guide to build something similar to this and other great projects for your backyard.

Figure Three: Grill and outdoor fireplace combo with a minibar, ideal for outdoor entertaining

Figure Four: Detail, the chimney

Figure Five: Side view of structure

Figure Six: Detail: Decorative arch

Figure Seven: Detail, light fixture and different stonework

The difference between mortar and concrete is crucial to know about when working with masonry. As mentioned in the last chapter you learned about mixing concrete, but mixing mortar is different. The key ingredients needed for mixing of mortar are listed below.

A. **Mortar mix** is key. For more artistic masonry, primarily the brands of LaFarge and Brixmath are the best. LaFarge is the mortar mix of choice for our jobs, but Brixmath can also work. LaFarge is a good brand because it gives a smooth feel to the mortar and makes it easier to handle. The key to making good mortar is to use the right mortar or cement mix. Cement mix has a special letter code which denotes how much Portland cement is in the mix. Portland cement is the active ingredient in all cement mixes, even the ready made mixes with the sand mixed in the bag, which by the way, we do not recommend. You're better off mixing your own mortar.

    11. **Type I** is the strongest mix for mortar. Typically Type I cement mix is primarily for mixing concrete, which needs to be super strong. Type I is about 100 percent Portland cement and Type I cement should only be used in mixing special mortars for fireplaces or

chimneys. You will learn this too. Type I mortar mix is also good for making the caps of chimneys for a type of grill or outdoor fireplaces as seen above.

12. **Type M** is a strong mortar mix and is ideal for outdoor masonry features. Type M mortar mix is typically a mixture of 75 percent Portland cement and 25 percent lime and other ingredients. Typically, Type M is used for cinderblock foundations of houses and cinderblock buildings. We like it for outdoor features, because it can handle the rigors of the winter cold very well.

13. **Type S** is the standard mortar mix which most contractors and bricklayers use. It is strong, but is not recommended to build a foundation. Type S mortar mix is about 50 percent Portland cement and 50 percent lime and other ingredients.

14. **Type N** should not be used in mixing mortar and should not be used outside. Type N is very weak cement mix with only 25 percent Portland cement and 75 percent other ingredients. Type N cement mix is mainly used in mixing grout for tile work.

B. **Mason sand** is the second ingredient in mixing mortar. As mentioned earlier, mason sand is sand taken from riverbeds. This is sand which can compact and is fine grain, making it ideal for mortar mix. The key function of the sand is to make the mortar porous and allows the mortar to breath. As a rule, you should use two shovels of mason sand to every one shovel of mortar mix.

C. **Water** to add the moisture to the mix. You want your mortar to have a good thick mud like consistency when you apply it to the sand and mortar mix. If the mortar starts to crumble, then add more water, if the mortar is too liquid, you should add another two parts sand and one part mortar. You want to be able to shape the mortar in your hand. It needs to be solid enough so you can pack it in cracks and between stones.

Tools needed for masonry are varied depending on the type of masonry you are doing. The basic tools are listed below.

Trowels are very important when it comes to masonry work. There is a wide variety of trowels and other tools available and are explained below.

A. **Mason or brick trowel** is what you typically think of when thinking of a trowel people use when working with mortar. As seen in Figure Eight below, the mason trowel is the triangular trowel. You can get large ones which are needed for bricklaying, but when working with stone, a small or medium sized mason trowel would be sufficient. This trowel does have a wide variety of uses, but it is primarily used to scoop mortar from the board.

B. **Slicker or tuck pointing trowels** are ideal for working with stone. Also shown in Figure Eight, these trowels are long slender trowels which are used frequently by tuck pointers. (see the epilogue in the maintenance section) When working with stone masonry, you are working with natural stone which can have organic or irregular shapes. This means that you will have gaps of different sizes which you will need to pack mortar in. These slicker trowels come in different sizes, some of which are almost wire thin and others can be as broad as a quarter inch. Have all the widths that are available as you will need a broader slicker trowel for wider gaps and thinner slicker trowels for narrower gaps. You can also use these slicker trowels to carefully do delicate work with mortar to make a flagstone wall look like a cut from a mountain side.

C. **Flat trowel** is a rectangular trowel which is mostly used for mixing smaller amounts of mortar. This trowel, also shown in Figure Eight, is also often used in making and applying fire mortar for grills, fireplaces, and fire pits.

D. **Masonry saw** to cut cinder blocks used in making the basic structure for an outdoor kitchen or entertaining area, fireplace, grill, or other outdoor feature. You can get a large mason saw, which professional bricklayers use, but those are very expensive. You can also rent them but you may have to replace the blade. You can also get masonry blades for your skill or miter saw at any Lowe's or Home Depot in the power tools section.

E. **Safety glasses and respirator** to wear when working with the mason saw. You may also want to wear safety glasses and respirator when mixing the dry elements of your mortar, as cement dust can affect people who have sensitive eyes and respiratory systems.

F. **Wheelbarrow or cement mixer** to mix your mortar. If you use a wheelbarrow, you want to make sure it's a stable one, ideally with two wheels, not one and a mortar hoe. (See the concrete section of Chapter Five)

Figure Eight: Different trowels used for stone masonry

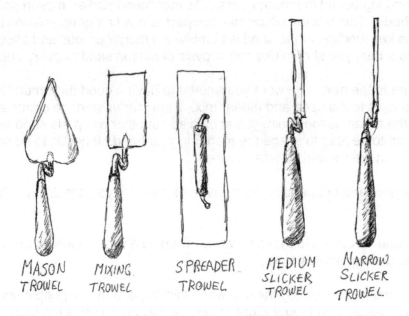

MASON TROWEL   MIXING TROWEL   SPREADER TROWEL   MEDIUM SLICKER TROWEL   NARROW SLICKER TROWEL

Proper storage of mason sand is key to having a good mortar mixture when you are working on your project. Most large masonry projects require mason sand to be delivered by the truckload. This means that you have to get the sand from a concrete vendor or landscape center which sells mason sand who can deliver it and drop it with a dump truck to your area. Ideally, you will want to have a large tarp or plastic on the ground where you want the sand to be delivered. This will keep weeds from the ground from growing into the sand. You want to avoid plant material from getting into your sand. Also you will want to cover your sand with a tarp from the top to keep weeds from seeding themselves in it. Even with the following measures mentioned in this paragraph, you may want to sift the sand with a fine sieve to filter out roots or other plant material which may have slipped through the cracks.

The best kinds of stone to get started with when you are new to masonry is either large fieldstone or medium sized slabs of flagstones. Fieldstone boulders are great to get started with as they are fairly large and look very nice. They can be easy to cement together and you can also place smaller stones in the larger gaps of the stone. Once you have mastered this art, the possibilities of what you can create are endless.

Slabs of flagstone are also great to work with. Flagstone may be flat and thin, but because they are wide, you can easily build a small retaining wall five to six feet which would safely hold to the pressure of pushing roots and other forces pushing the soil against it. Higher retaining walls should have a backing of cinderblocks with support rods cemented in some of the holes of the blocks for extra support on taller walls. You will learn this later in this chapter.

Figure Nine: Basic mortaring of fieldstone

Use the large mason trowel to scoop up the mortar and place it above the stone. Use the slicker trowels to push the mortar tightly into the cracks.

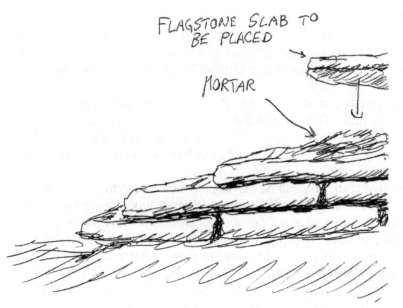

Figure Ten: Basic mortaring of flagstone slabs

When mortaring flagstone slabs together, you may be dealing with large slabs, thus use your spreader trowel to give a good coat of mortar on the top of the slab. Once the second layer is placed, then use the slicker trowel to push any excess mortar into the cracks between the slabs and compact it in for good adhesion.

Adding color to your masonry can also add some character to your work. If you have artistic skill and learn the basics of masonry mentioned above, you can literally make features around your flowerbeds, water gardens and waterfalls, or other landscape features look like completely natural mountain features.

The right way to color your mortar is not by getting the liquid colors made by Quickcrete brand sold at Lowe's or Home Depot. Though many people use these liquid colors, they are problematic, as they will make your mortar too watery and you will have to add more one part mortar mix and two parts sand to get the right consistency.

Professionals never use liquid colors when adding color to mortars. Most professionals will order mortar color in powder form. Why is powder pigment better than the liquid pigment you can get at the big-box stores? Well, the answer to that is quite simple. The liquid colors which are intended for the average do-it-yourselfers are only four colors, black, terra cotta, red, and yellow. These colors are limiting and there is a reason why these are the only colors available. Other colors, such as blues and greens can get very expensive, especially when made in liquid form.

Where does mortar coloring come from? Well, mortar coloring comes from a wide variety of mineral and metal oxides. Depending on the metal or mineral, the oxides can be very cheap or very expensive. Here is a list of different mortar colors available in powder form and what metals or minerals they come from. You will also see a ballpark figure of how much you can expect to pay for a basic five pound bag of these colors. Below you will also learn where you can apply and mix all these different colors.

A. **Black** is typically from aluminum oxide. Aluminum will turn black when oxidized rapidly, like with fire or other oxidizing agent. Aluminum is rather inexpensive and for a five pound bag of black mortar coloring powder you can expect to pay around 20 dollars. The prices will vary from brand to brand.

B. **Terra cotta, red, orange** are all varieties of iron oxides. Basically, reds and oranges, including terra cotta, are powdered rust. The color of the iron oxide can vary from the type of iron is being oxidized. Iron oxides are relatively inexpensive and a five pound bag of red, terra cotta, or orange can range anywhere from $10 to $30 per five pound bag. Some reds can be a mix of iron and other oxides also.

C. **Green** is one of the most expensive color you will be buying. There is a wide variety of green colors available, such as slate color, emerald green, and other types of darker greens. The primary ingredient for green mortar color is copper oxide. Copper is very expensive and the more green or brighter green you buy, the more copper oxide is in the mix, thus the more you can expect to pay per five pound bag. Other darker greens, such as green slate, Pennsylvania green (mimicking a green shale quarried in Pennsylvania), or other like stone color will be a mix of copper, aluminum, and other different mineral and metal oxides. For any green color, you can expect to pay from $60 to $100 per five pound bag.

D. **Yellow** can be from a wide variety of different oxides. Yellow comes from so many different mineral oxides which are readily available, so this is one of the more inexpensive colors on the market. For a five pound bag of yellow, expect to pay ten to twenty dollars.

The above mentioned colors are the most common colors available at most masonry specialty places. You can also get a color chart from these masonry stores and if they do not have a particular color, they can order it for you or direct you to a website where you can order from.

Mixing mortar color with your mortar mix is rather simple. Simply add the powder to your mortar mix and sand after you add water. You may have to add extra water as the powder can dry your mixture as you mix it in. Since most of the mortar colors are mineral or metal oxides, they are much finer than mason sand, so they will not phase the consistency of nor the effectiveness of the bond of your mortar. Don't be afraid to mix different colors in the same batch to create your own colors when adding color to your mortar.

Using Cinderblocks and Natural Stone Together

If you want to have a fancy backyard with all the bells and whistles, but don't want to pay thousands of dollars to a contractor to do it for you, you can actually do it yourself and have the same results.

When building outdoor kitchens, bars, minibars, grills, fireplaces, and the like, you will need to have a solid structure to build from. Thus using cinderblocks is a necessity when building these structures. Cinderblocks are rather inexpensive and you can even cut cost in purchasing cinderblocks if you find a manufacturer who makes them on site.

Many cinderblock manufacturers will actually have cinderblocks that may have a small esthetic defect which will not allow them to sell them to local masonry stores, contractors, or stone yards. These blocks are perfectly fine, but they will sell them at a discounted price. Some will also have a scrapyard where they will throw away cinderblocks or other concrete construction products away, which they cannot sell. Some factories will even let you come into those scrapyards and take what you want for free. Some of them are happy to have you do that, as it will reduce their cost in disposing of them.

Check local building codes and zoning ordinances before you start any large undertaking involving cinderblocks. Many communities, counties, and homeowner associations will require some kind of permit when building large structures, such as fireplaces, grills, or entertainment areas. At times, you may even have to add electricity for lights, stereos, or refrigerators for your backyard entertainment area, thus this can also cause an issue with some municipalities. Some states may also have requirements for permits for any kind of fire containing structure, even those as simple as a fire pit. The best way to find out what permits you will need is to go to your town or city hall and talk to the clerk. Typically the clerk will have all the information you will need and can direct you to the right department.

Basic tools needed when building with cinderblocks. Besides a good masonry saw, a good set of tools needed for work with cinderblocks is much like those needed for bricklaying. This is because building with cinderblocks is just like bricklaying, but on a larger scale. These basic tools and supplies are listed below.

A. **Water levels** are necessary to make sure that your structure is level and the vertical walls are plum. Water levels are typically in a wooden or metal bar and have a diagonal, horizontal, and vertical glass tube with some colored water with enough airspace to have a bubble. These glass tubes have two markings on them and when the air bubble in the water is within the two marks,then your surface is level. You can also get a small water level which is attached to a string. Use this kind of level to set string in a level fashion as a guide to lay the blocks.

B. **Metal mallet or small sledgehammer** to pound reebarb or other support metal rods to add strength to the structure. This is especially crucial for building retaining walls which are ten feet or higher. These support rods need also to be used when building outdoor fireplaces or entertainment areas, especially when flowerbeds are between masonry walls.

C. **Above mentioned trowels** to pack the mortar tightly between the blocks to make a solid bond.

Adding electrical features in masonry structures can be a bit tricky, so this should be done gradually. If you need to burry wire or have it go in around and organic form, conduit may not be an option. We recommend that you have a licensed electrician install the circuit breaker to the wire and show you how to turn it on and off. Then with the instructions here, you can install the electrical features by yourself rather easily. Simply keep the circuit breaker off before you complete the structure and all electrical features are safely installed. In the series of figures below, you will see how you can run wire and mortar electrical boxes in your structure. Later in this chapter, you will also see how to wire in electrical outlets, outdoor light switches, and lighting fixtures.

Figure Eleven: See how the wire comes up from its hole into the block structure.

See how you can simply place a block carefully and run the wire through one of the two holes in the block. Keep repeating this process until you reach the area where the outlet, switch, or fixture box needs to be cemented in.

Figure Twelve: Installing the electrical box, rectangular for switches and outlets and round for a light fixture.

Notice that if you need to continue wiring from the boxes, simply repeat the process by running more wire through. If you need to run wire horizontally between layers of blocks, you can simply carefully chisel an indentation in the with-span of the block wide enough to allow the wire to go through unimpeded.

When building your basic cinderblock structure, you want to think about cementing in binders to help strengthen the bond of the stone vernier to the block structure. These binders are small pieces of corrugated galvanized metal which are designed to bond with mortared vernier to cinderblocks or to chickenwire stapled to wood structures, like the side of a house. These binders can be bent as needed.

Verniering your block structure with natural stone is very simple, but it can be time consuming. Simply mortar the stone to the blocks as shown in Figure Thirteen.

Figure Thirteen: The process of stone vernier on the cinderblock structure.

Fire Brick and Fire Clay
If you are planning to build a grill, fireplace, or fire pit, you will want to use fire bricks and a heat proof mortar mix. This can be difficult to do, as fire mortar can be very difficult to handle when it is wet. It also cures much slower than regular mortar. In fact, fire mortar can stay soft for up to ten days or more, depending on the humidity of the ambient air.

Why the need for fire brick and fire cement? Fires, like the one in your fire pit, grill, or fireplace can get very hot. Some fires can get up to 700 to one thousand degrees Fahrenheit and this can be stress on cinderblocks and regular mortar, even mortar with Type I mix. The heat of a fire can transform the molecular structure of both the cinderblocks and the mortar holding the blocks together. In fact, if you have ever gone to the beach or camping and used a couple of old cinderblocks to hold spits for shish-kebabs or a grate for hotdogs or hamburgers, you notice that the blocks have developed cracks? Sometimes, the blocks may even break it two. This is why you need fire brick and mortar.

The makeup of fire bricks is a special clay which when fired is a light yellow in color. This hard fired clay is not only strong enough to withstand heat up to 2,500 degrees Fahrenheit, which is common in most industrial grade kilns, but also insulate the outer structure from that damaging heat. In fact most fire bricks you buy are made to build kilns, so most of them can withstand intense heat.

Making fire cement or mortar is a complex process. Fire cement is often called fire clay, however, fire clay is only one ingredient in fire cement. Basically, to make fire cement, you do the same mortar mix that you do for regular mortar, but you add the Type I pure Portland cement as the cement mix and add the fire clay. Basically, fire clay is actually a clay which hardens and when fired, mixes well with mortars and makes a strong bond between the fire bricks and will not break apart when it gets hot.

One of the reasons why fire cement stays soft for such a long time is because of the fire clay. Clay will slowly release moisture, thus you want to wait, sometimes a whole month after mortaring your grill before starting a fire. This will be discussed a bit later.

Heatstop is a better alternative to mixing your own fire cement. Heatstop is fire cement, but it is already mixed by professionals who know the right consistency. Heatstop can be bought in two different forms, first in plastic buckets where when you pop the lid, it is ready to use. You can also buy it in a 15 pound bag in powder form and all you need to do is add water and you are ready to go. Heatstop is one of America's top brands of fire cement and many masonry contractors use it. The drawback of Heatstop is that it is very messy to work with and it will stick to your trowels. It is very difficult to wash off and you will want to keep your trowels fairly wet when working with Heatstop to keep it from sticking to your trowels. Also, keep Heatstop from coming into contact with your bare skin or clothes, because it is very abrasive. When using Heatstop, you will notice that it has a very strong bond, even when wet, thus when you put the fire bricks together, you may not be able to get them apart again, so apply with care.

Laying fire brick is basically like laying regular brick, but you are using special bricks and special cement. Use a water level to check if the bricks are level and you should also make sure your level is made of something which does not stick to cement, as fire cement or Heatstop can be very difficult to get off, especially after it dried. When adding the fire brick, you want to just put it in the area where you will have your fires, as both fire bricks and Heatstop are very expensive.

When laying fire brick inside your grill, fireplace, or fire pit, add a hefty gob of Heatstop between each brick and between the back of the brick and the cinderblock structure. Hot air can expand, so you do not want air pockets in the fire area. See Figure Fourteen below to see how to properly lay fire bricks in your fire area against the main block structure.

Figure Fourteen:
Installation of fire bricks

Notice that the space between the firebricks which is filled with the Heatstop or other type of fire mortar needs to be much narrower and thinner to reduce the risk of air bubbles forming in the fire cement used in the project. You should also use fire mortar or Heatstop between the firebrick and cinderblock wall.

Chimney liners (for outdoor fireplaces) can be bought at any masonry store which carries fire bricks and fire cement supplies. Unlike fire bricks, which are a light yellow, chimney liners are more of a brownish terra cotta color. These are also heat resistant, but they are not as strong as the fire bricks. Typically, chimney liners can withstand heat up to 1,500 degrees Fahrenheit. They do not need to be as strong as the bricks, as the heat is not as intense in the chimney as where the fire is. You do need a heat resistant liner in the chimney nonetheless, because if you build a good enough fire, fire might sometimes shoot out of the chimney.

Use fire cement or Heatstop to mortar the sections of chimney liner together or to the top of the fireplace, but you can use regular Type I mortar to vernier the natural stone around the chimney liner.

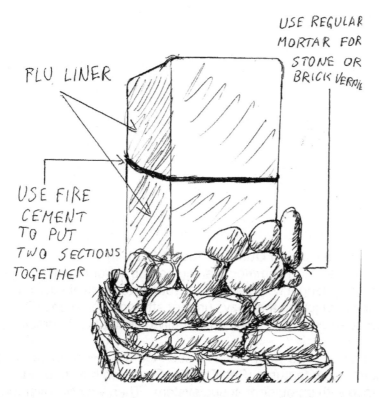

Figure Fifteen: Flue liner and stone vernier being mortared around it.

Use of Boulders as Accents in your Landscaping

Boulders can always make a statement in any landscaping design. Some boulders are huge and can be up to three feet tall, others are smaller. Most boulders are brought from fields where farmers dig them up and want to get rid of them. Many landscape stores will contract with local farmers to get the boulders and sell them at a marked up price in their yards. Some stone yards will carry boulders from all over the country, and you can choose them also.

Great ideas for boulders include being a centerpiece for flower islands in a lawn setting, masking rock speakers of an outdoor sound system, and more. See Figure Sixteen for ideas on positioning boulders in your yard.

Figure Sixteen: Boulder positioning on the landscape layout

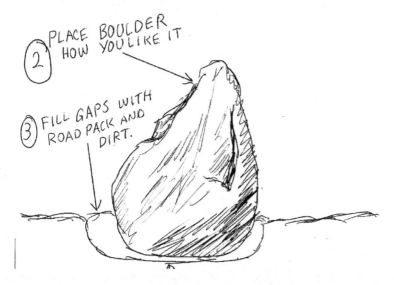

Building the Ultimate Entertainment Area with an Outdoor Sound System
How nice it would be to have some of those warm summer evening parties in your own landscape design or sitting back, grilling, getting a cold beer out of your outdoor minibar, and listening to your favorite music and simply enjoying that lazy summer afternoon or evening? Well, with all the information you have learned above, you can actually build that up yourself.

Before we get started with the tools and materials you need, lets see Figure Seventeen below to show a layout which includes a minibar, water features (See Chapter Seven on how to build those) Outdoor fireplace and grill combo with an outdoor sound system. Then we will cover the details on how to install the electrical fixtures, rock speakers, and choosing your stereo system. We will also talk about the right refrigerator for the outdoor minibar and how to maintain it so it won't break down in the winter months.

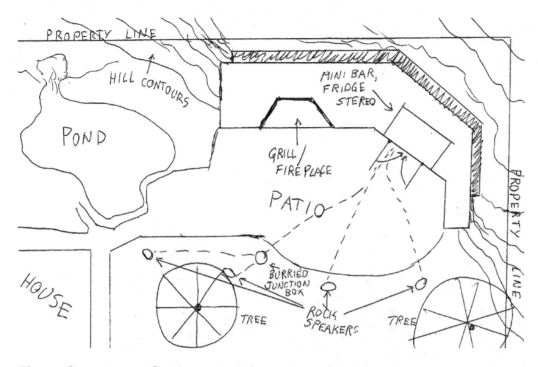

Figure Seventeen: Outdoor entertainment area layout

Installing electrical outlets is the easiest thing to do. As you saw in the above section about building with cinderblocks, the box is already cemented in and the wires are sticking out. Go to any Lowe's, Home Depot, or other home improvement store and find in the electrical department a regular grounded electrical outlet. If you did not have your electrician installed a GFCI circuit breaker (recommended), then you should get GFCI electrical outlets. A GFCI circuit will automatically trip and shut off any power should moisture get into the receptacle, preventing electric shock. If you have a GFCI circuit breaker, then you do not need GFCI outlets. If not, then only one GFCI outlet is enough, as the outlet itself has a mini circuit breaker in it, so all the other plugs will be cut off as well.

Along with the electrical outlets, get special outdoor outlet plates. These have caps with a weatherproof seal which close over the receptacle, keeping rain water out. If the outlets are designed to keep a pump plugged in for your pond or water feature, you can get special plates with a hood that protect the plug from the cord and the receptacle.

As seen in Figure Eighteen below, installing an electrical outlet will not disrupt the flow of electricity and you can have several outlets in one circuit. You simply want to make sure that the circuit has strong enough to pull enough amperage for everything you want, stereo, refrigerator, etc. A 20 ampre circuit breaker should do the job.

When installing an electrical outlet, all you need to do is to shave away the weatherproof insulation from both wires or in some cases three wires in the box. When you peal back the weatherproof insulation, you will notice three wires. One will have white insulation, the other black, and one will be naked. The naked wire is ground, black is hot, and the white is the return current. Simply place the black wire on the brass screws of the outlet, the white wires on the silver screws, the naked wire gets screwed to the screw on the box and on the green screw on the receptacle. The weatherproof plate has a single screw which you can screw into the outlet. The outlet gets screwed into place in two screws to the top and bottom of the box.

Figure Eighteen: Installing an outlet with a basic outdoor plate

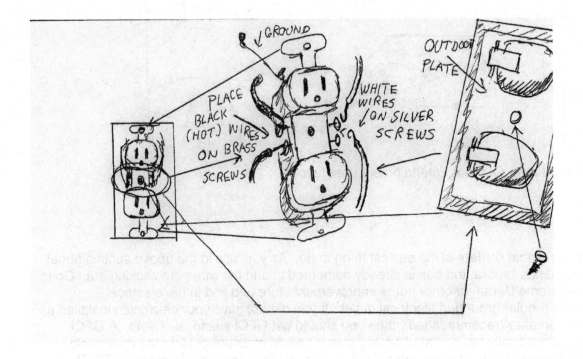

Notice the positioning of the wires, how to secure the receptacle, and fastening the plate.

You may want to get some silicone sealant to seal the plate to the box to prevent moisture from coming into the box. You may also want to put a healthy gob of silicone in the holes where the wires come into the box.

Installing a light switch outside is a bit different from inside. Though wiring it in the box is the same, the plate is different. You can get a hooded plate where you lift the hood to get to the switch. This will allow you to access the switch to turn on a light, but at the same time, it will protect the toggle of the switch from the elements. Wiring a switch is very simple. See Figure Nineteen below.

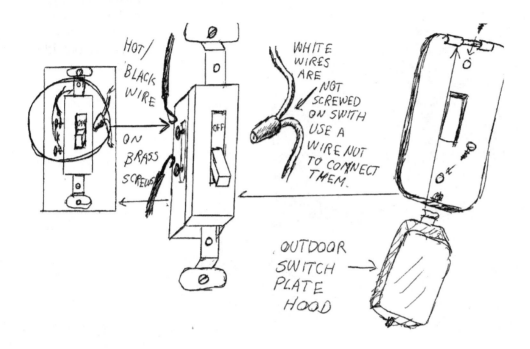

Figure Nineteen: Installing a regular light switch

Note that installing a light switch is different from an outlet. The switch only has two brass screws for the hot wires. There is a reason for this. The white wire is not always hot. In fact, if you have nothing plugged in and all the lights are off, you can touch the white wire and not get a shock. This is because the white wire just brings the current back, closing the circuit. The black wire, however, is always hot. That wire is not to be touched, so for God's sake, when installing any electrical fixture, be it an outlet, switch, or light fixture, make sure the circuit breaker is off.

Installing a switch with an indicator light can be handy for your fridge. Most minibar refrigerators are small two foot tall and will pull at most one to three ampres. The indicator switch fits into a plate for a wall outlet, but you wire the switch just like you would a normal switch, but you add the wiring to the indicator light. This will make the indicator light turn on when the switch is on. This can be handy, because you will know if the power to the fridge is on or not.

Installing a light fixture is very easy. Simply choose a light fixture you want to install, take it out of the box, and connect the wires with wire nuts. It's that simple. Make sure the wires match. Most light fixtures will have a black wire for hot, white for the negative, and a naked or green for ground. The ground always gets wired to the box.

When installing a light fixture, you want to make sure you have a round box which has enough space to hold all the wiring. See Figure Twenty below on how to wire a light fixture.

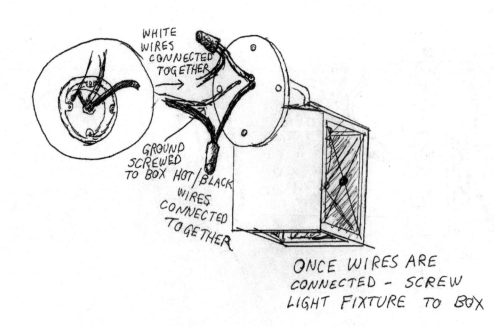

Figure Twenty: Installing a light fixture to your masonry outside walls

ONCE WIRES ARE CONNECTED - SCREW LIGHT FIXTURE TO BOX

Note, you should always seal the holes where the wires come in and the area around the light fixture with silicone to prevent moisture from coming in.

Installing the sound system is tricky. You will need to choose speakers which are designed to be installed outside. There are many speakers made for outside. Some can be affixed to your house, others are shaped like boulders and blend with real boulders very well.

The basics in choosing your speakers and stereo can be a bit on the complicated side. Though Lowe's, Home Depot, and Walmart may have rock speakers for sale in their electrical or outdoor electrical departments, you will have to read the specs of the speakers on the box before you purchase them from there. A better idea is to go to a specialty store which is specifically devoted to electronics and audio equipment. There, a salesman who is knowledgeable of the stereos and speakers available can explain what stereo is compatible with what speaker. Basic things to look for are listed below.

A. **How many ohms can your speaker handle?** Ohms are a unit of measure for low voltage electricity which goes into your speakers when your stereo is playing. This is what causes your speakers to make the sound audible. The higher the ohms your speakers can take, the more the sound output from your stereo can be amplified. Furthermore, if your stereo puts out more ohms than your speakers can take, it can blow out your speakers and they will then be irreparably damaged. It is always good to have your speakers handle more ohms than your stereo can put out.

B. **How many feet of cable** can be used to maximize the performance of your speakers. Because speakers use a lower current than regular electrical appliances, cable length can cause problems, especially for lower quality speakers. If you have a high quality sound system with surround sound, you will want to get all your speakers in a circle around the outdoor entertainment area so you and your guests can enjoy the sound. Ideally, speakers should keep their optimum performance with up to 100 feet of cable or more.

Choosing the right stereo sound unit and proper storage of it is important also. Today, we have a wide variety of different sound devices from iPods and MP3 players to the late 20th Century compact disks. You want to have a system which can play all of these. When choosing one with a CD player, you want to make sure it's a high quality brand, as the lasers of CD players can burn out and this will then prevent the player from reading your CDs.

Keeping your stereo should be in a cabinet inside your minibar which protects it from the elements and keeps it dry. Moisture and water condensation can fry out the circuitry of your sound system.

Laying sound cable for your outdoor speakers needs to forego serious planning. You want to plan this while you are building your minibar. Have a conduit pipe run under any concrete slabs so your cable can get from the speakers to the back of your sound unit. If there is long conduit, you can attach a small piece of cork to thin string and tie the other end of the string to the cable. Use an air compressor to shoot the cork tied to the string through the pipe. It will come out on the other side, then gently pull the string until the cable gets to the outside end of the pipe.

You will want to dig trenches about three inches deep to lay the cable. You also want to make sure the speaker cable you get is good for outdoor use. If not, you can still use it, but it will have to be in conduit pipe. You can use regular PVC pipe for conduit.

Use round light fixture boxes to connect the cables. The cables can be connected with wire nuts and electrical tape. Make sure none of the separate wires have the naked parts contact each other. Audio signal will not be delivered to the speaker if this happens. This is why it's so important to over tape the connections with electrical tape, as electrical tape can insulate.

Position the speakers where you want them and then go back to the stereo cabinet and connect the cable to the stereo's output plugins. Most stereos will have red grippers which lock for the red wire and black for the black wire. Make sure the wires are plugged in securely and test the speakers. If all sounds good, bury the cables and you're set. See Figure Twenty-One for a configuration of your speakers.

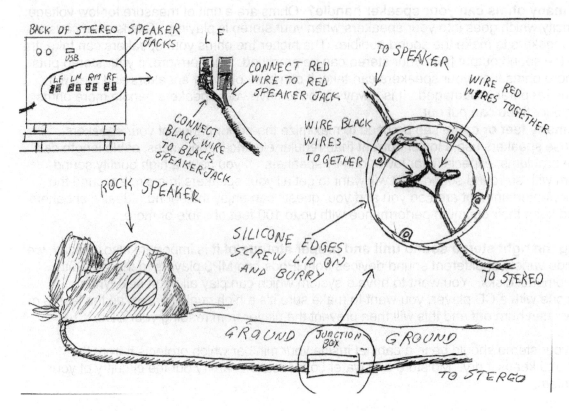

Labels in figure:
BACK OF STEREO SPEAKER JACKS
USB
LF LM RM RF
LF
CONNECT RED WIRE TO RED SPEAKER JACK
CONNECT BLACK WIRE TO BLACK SPEAKER JACK
ROCK SPEAKER
TO SPEAKER
WIRE RED WIRES TOGETHER
WIRE BLACK WIRES TOGETHER
SILICONE EDGES SCREW LID ON AND BURRY
TO STEREO
GROUND   JUNCTION BOX   GROUND
TO STEREO

Figure Twenty-One: See how speakers, cable, and stereo are connected together.

Now, you have all the knowledge on how to build the backyard of your dreams, go ahead and do it and start having years of good summer fun in your new back yard.

Chapter Seven

Water gardening and Water Features

Adding a water feature or water garden to your landscape can make it a place of serenity and tranquility. Whether you want a fishpond full of koi and other goldfish for the kids or simply whether you want to have a simple water feature which is low maintenance, we can show you how to do it.

In this chapter you will learn everything which has to do with water gardening and special water features. You will also learn how you can incorporate water fountains and waterfalls with ponds, and more. This chapter will be broken down as follows:

A. The basics of water gardening and what to choose. What is water gardening, and all the aspects of water gardening, such as pond building, hardscaping, low maintenance fountains, and bog gardens. Why people like water gardens and water features in their landscaping. We will also cover the history of water gardening, and give ideas for fishponds, reflecting ponds, and basic water features and fountains.

B. **Pond building** and what supplies are needed for pond building. Masonry ponds versus ponds with loose stone, designing your own pond. This will be the longest segment of this chapter and you will learn how to neutralize the Ph of the water in masonry ponds and make it fish friendly. Some of the techniques for both creating, stocking, and maintenance are listed below.

    15. **Basic supplies** needed to build your pond. What is pond rubber, building a customized pond versus a pond with a solid shaped liner, how to build masonry ponds using rubber pond liner and make it stick.

    16. **Making your masonry pond fish friendly** is crucial if you want your fish to survive. You will learn why mortar in masonry makes the water a high Ph level. How to neutralize it with vinegar and prepare the water for fish.

    17. **Varieties of pond fish** for your pond. The fish we primarily will be talking about are decorative carp, such as goldfish, fantails, shubunkins, and koi. Proper care and feeding of pond fish. The importance of water aeration and filtration for fish.

    18. **Biologically maintaining your pond** to make your pond as much of a natural environment as possible.

    19. **How to properly stock your pond with fish** and isolate diseased fish.

C. **Water features for ponds** and how you can make your pond an amazing attraction for your backyard.

D. **Water plants** for your pond or bog garden. This segment will cover water lilies, water iris, underwater plants, water vines, and floating plants (water annuals), such as water hyacinths and water lettuce.

E. **Low maintenance water features,** such as fountains without ponds. Learn how to build a fairly inexpensive garbage can fountain, hardscaping, what it is and how it can transform any wall in your yard, including walls on your house.

F. **Making complex water features** by having a powerful pump for circulation or even several pumps, build your own flow control manifolds, and learn about different types of fountain heads.

The Basics of Water gardening

Water gardens have been a huge part of civilization for thousands of years. Many cultures have used ponds and water fountains to add serenity and tranquility to their gardens. The ancient Romans were very sophisticated when it came to making water features. Their advanced engineering skills for that period has proven to be phenomenal. They were able to build water falls and features by using gravity and taping into mountain streams. The Japanese mastered hybridizing carp and adorned their ponds with one of the most popular species of decorative carp today, koi. Chinese, Europeans, and India have also used reflecting ponds throughout their landscape.

Water gardening can be very high maintenance when it comes to fishponds but the results can also be very rewarding. If that high maintenance is not your cup of tea, there are water gardens for you also. You can hardscape and build a simple wall fountain which spits water out into a catch basin and circulates with a pump. You can also have amazing geyser fountains using, what we affectionately call a garbage can fountain, which is where a plastic garbage can or larger fire barrel is used as the catch basin and is covered with a screen lid covered with pebbles.

If you love water plants but hate fishing out leaves and dead plant matter from a pond, then a bog garden might be the right thing for you. Bog gardens are literally a swamp garden. These are ideal for water iris, elephant ears, canna lilies, and other bog plants.

Pond Building

When it comes to having water gardens, ponds are by far the most popular. This is why we devote most of this chapter on building the right pond. When building a pond, there is so much involved, such as layout, depth of the pond, what kind of water features you want, and more. Of course, there are the fish. Most ponds are not complete without being fully stocked with fish.

The basics of building your own pond can be done in several ways. If you want to have a small fish pond with some small goldfish, you can get forms from Lowe's or Home Depot, but those can be very limiting and they can be very difficult to cover. The better alternative is to go to a special landscaping store or nursery which has a pond department. They sell special rubber which is very thick and hard to puncture. High quality roofing rubber used for flat roofs can also work well.

Digging your pond has to be carefully planned out and if not done properly, it can cause the pond to loose water rapidly. Also, some communities may require permits to build ponds which are deeper than six feet and may require you to build a fence around those larger ponds, like you have to in a swimming pool in most areas. Ideally, you would want to dig your pond at the bottom of a hill where the ground is rather flat. You can also dig your pond in the side of a hill, as long as it is at the foot of the hill. Doing that can make for some interesting water features.

Shallow sloped banks versus steep sloped banks is also something to think about. If you want a fishpond and plan to have other decorative carp, besides the basic goldfish, you will want to have steep banks around your pond instead shallow banks. The reason for this is that popular fish, such as koi are very expensive at $40 per fish or more, depending on the breed. Fish also attract predators, such as cats, both domesticated and ferrel, raccoons, and birds. We will talk about predators and how to repel them later. Raccoons and cats can be the biggest problem, but if the banks are steep to an almost vertical drop, they will have a hard time catching your prize fish. Raccoons like shallow slopes where they can simply wade in and wait for fish to swim to their reach.

Methods of pond construction can also differ depending on how you want to build your pond. The two types of construction are listed below.

A. **Loose stone construction** is ideal for shallow sloped banks. With loose stone construction, mortaring is not necessary and you can even add sand to cover the pond rubber, just make sure that there is rubber above the water level of the pond, to ensure there is no leakage. Most pond builders who build ponds with loose stone will use a mixture of sand and river rock for the bottom, so it is easier to plant water plants and flowers. You can also add larger stones, such as fieldstone, flagstone, or other decorative boulders to create the affect you desire. A caveat with limestone slabs. Limestone is very alkaline, so you will have to take Ph tests of the water and neutralize the Ph level of the water before stocking it with fish.

B. **Mortared or cement ponds** are more durable and can allow you to create all kinds of different features, such as mimicking fault lakes with steep banks to ponds looking like they are in a mountainous or rocky terrain. If you want to let your imagination go wild, then masonry is the way to go. Doing a mortared or cement pond is much like doing basic masonry, but some additional things need to be done, which are listed below.

1. **Line the rubber with chickenwire** before adding any stone. The pond rubber will not bond with mortar or concrete, so you will have to use the chickenwire to mortar all the stones together. You can then backfill the stone walls with concrete to make a strong and solid side of your pond and ensure it will not crack with freezing water in the wintertime.
2. **Use concrete on the bottom of the pond** to help make a base for the pond walls.

Tips on digging your pond will be shown in Figures One and Two below. Basically, soil types are different throughout the US. Along the shores of the Great Lakes, such as Lakes Michigan, Huron, and Erie, the soil is very sandy, but further away you have a stronger rocky and clay soil, which can be harder to dig in. Sandy soil is very easy to dig in, but sand can move and once the sand dries, it will fall partly back in the hole.

If you live in more mountainous areas, your soil can be very rocky and you may even have to rent a jackhammer to loosen bigger stones for your pond. Depending on your area, some ground beds can hold water better than others, but nonetheless, you should have pond rubber to line the pond before beginning to build up stone and sand around it. Different types of soil bases and how they hold water are listed below.

A. **Sand** is very porous and will not hold water at all. If you live in a sandy area, you will want to have a good rubber lining installed after digging your pond. Sand can also shift, so you want to make sure your water features and pipes are set in special concrete casing so they won't erode the sand should they leak. If your area has sand dunes with trees, like most of lower Michigan around the Great Lakes, you will want to build a strong retaining wall at the back of your pond before adding the rubber. You can even build a ridge on which you can weigh the rubber down with heavy stones before you have a chance to add the chickenwire and do any mortaring. (On the side of a hill or sand dune, you should use masonry as it will hold better.

B. **Clay rocky sand** holds water a bit better than regular sand, but water will eventually sift through and your pond will dry out if you don't line it with rubber. Clay rocky sand will not erode as quickly as regular sand either.

C. **Limestone areas** where you are near a mountain range or at the foothills of one can hold water for a long time. Use a rubber lining anyway to hod water so you won't need to refill it often. This type of terrain is found in many parts of the US and Canada, such as central and southern Indiana, Kentucky, parts of southern Ohio, Pennsylvania, New York, Missouri, Tennessee, and other states.

D. **Rocky dessert areas,** like the American southwest might cause the water to hold for a while, but it will evaporate. In those areas, the sand instantly becomes clay when it gets wet, hence the cracks in the ground. Even with pond rubber lining (recommended), you want to make sure you have an automatic water delivery system to refill your pond in the hot summer months.

E. **Mountainous terrain** as found in Utah, Colorado, parts of Pennsylvania and New York, Missouri, Arkansas, California, Washington, Idaho, Montana, and other mountainous areas in the US and Canada, like Alberta and Saskatchewan can be very tricky to dig your pond. The problem in these areas is that there is rock and tough rocky sand. You may just start digging and you could hit a large slab of stone would impede your project. Here is where you may need a jackhammer to go through the stone. A word to the wise, only rent a jackhammer if you are strong enough to handle it. These machines have a lot of power and can do some bodily harm if not used or held correctly. If you do not feel comfortable using a jackhammer, hire a professional to do this job. This type of terrain does hold water quite well, but some of these areas, like Utah have predominantly sandstone terrain, which is porous so always use pond rubber.

Figure One: Digging a shallow pond with gradual shallow slopes

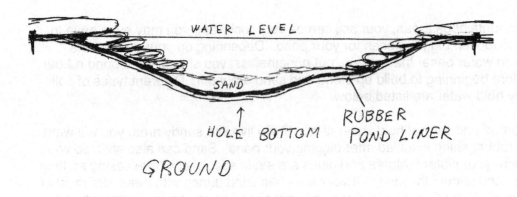

Figure Two: Digging a deep pond with steep slopes at the banks

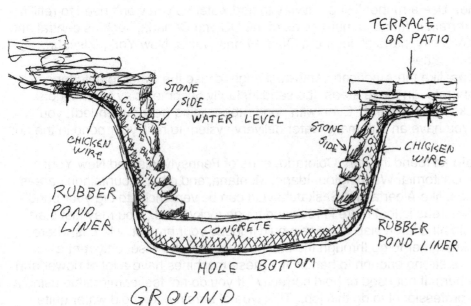

Cementing your pond is by far the best way to build your pond. Unfortunately, few landscapers who build ponds will use masonry, because it can be time consuming or it is very expensive because of the hard and tedious work it takes to build a cement and stone pond.

Figure Three will show how you need to prep your pond after you placed the rubber in the hole. When choosing your rubber, you want to know what the total volume of your future pond will be. Measure your pond's bottom and the approximate height of the pond walls. You should get enough rubber to cover the whole pond in one sheet. The reason for this is because the kits available to glue two sheets of pond rubber together are very expensive and if not glued properly, they will cause leaks. Rubber cement needs to be applied on a clean surface free of dirt, sand, or dust and there must be ample exposure in hot sun for the bond to dry and cure properly to have the necessary watertight seal. Avoid the problem all together by buying extra rubber. If you have too much excess, you can always cut the extra off.

Figure Three: Prepping your pond hole for mortaring stone

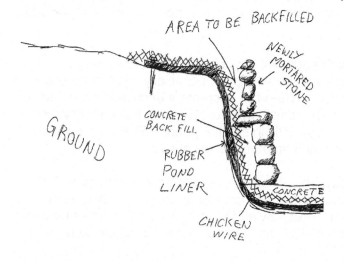

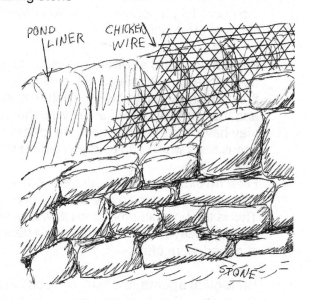

Notice how the chickenwire is laid right on the rubber. Try to have some space between the chickenwire and the rubber. This will allow you to reach behind the chickenwire and make sure the mortar will cover both sides of the wire. Also, notice that poured concrete on the bottom of the pond provides the right base for the stonework. If you are building a deep pond or a koi pond big enough to swim in, then place chickenwire a couple of feet so you can reach behind the stones. You can then back fill the walls with concrete. The weight of the concrete will also hold the rubber in place against the bare ground, so you won't have to worry about rubber sipping around and causing water loss. It is also a good idea that you backfill the stone walls with concrete for a stronger pond. Wait before a section you have mortared is hard before you backfill.

Preparing the water for fish is difficult and there are many things on the market to help make your water harmless for fish. Any pond made from masonry or having large limestone slabs or boulders in them will have to be made neutral before you can add fish to it. Do this by adding a gallon of vinegar to every five gallons of water, so for a 1500 gallon pond, you will need 300 gallons of vinegar to neutralize the water. You will not really smell the vinegar, as it will be neutralized just as the lime from the cement or limestone will be. Within a couple of days, the water Ph level should be around a six or seven, which is where you want it for fish.

Have the water features and the filter fully functioning when you add the vinegar to neutralize the water. This will ensure even movement of the water and all of it will then become a neutral Ph level.

Cleaning the tap water which comes out of your garden hose is also very important. Many cities and towns include chlorine, fluoride, and chloramine in their city water. These chemicals are extremely harmful to fish, so you will want to get it out of the water before stocking it. There are many products available both online and in specialty pond shops which can help you remove these harmful chemicals from your pond water. These are one-time drop chemicals and you only have to use them when you add fresh water. This is a special solution which breaks down the chlorine, fluoride, or chloramine molecules in the water, in effect neutralizing their harmful properties. Once you have followed these simple steps, then you are ready to add fish and other pond life.

Filter media and aerators are very crucial for the survival of your fish. Fish, especially decorative carp, (covered in the next paragraph) can be very dirty, especially if you over feed them. Fish excrement is your fishes worst enemy. When fish excrement decays in the water and there is lack of oxygen, it will generate into ammonia, which can kill your fish instantly. You may have to constantly measure for ammonia, especially in smaller ponds. There are special litmus tests which can help you determine how much ammonia is in your water.

Filter media comes in all different forms. Ideally, you will want a coarse polyester foam which has very rough and coarse to the touch. It tends to look like tangled threads in a whole sheet. This is the best filter media as it will not impede water flow and will trap all the fish excrement as well as decayed plant matter. More dense filter media can clog much faster and will have to be changed more often.

Biological agents to clean your pond are also available and do a much better job than chemicals. One biological brand available is Microbelift. This is manufactured by Ecological Laboratories, Inc in New York State. This is the top selling brand of biological agents and many pond contractors use their Microbelift product line for both prepping and maintenance of the ponds.

These biological solutions can do everything from killing off mosquito larvae before they mature to eating away decaying leaf litter and dead plant matter as well as messy pond sludge. In fact, if you use biological agents, like Microbelift, you will have to change your filters less often as the bacteria will colonize the filter media and help dissolve the sludge that fills up the filter. These biological agents literally eat the sludge in your filter.

Biological agents do not necessarily refer just to bacteria in solutions, like Microbelift, but plants and animals which you can get from wild ponds also. These are listed below.

A. **Water snails** are great for your pond. They will not be like regular snails or slugs which will come out on dry land and eat away at your flowers and landscape plants. Water snails will only survive in the water and they typically stay on the pond's bottom and sides eating away at the fish excrement and decaying sludge which the filter does not get.
B. **Freshwater muscles and clams** are a natural filter. They eat all the microscopic excrement from your fish.
C. **Pocostomous,** which is a type of bottom feeding fish will also help clean some of the sludge and algae that forms in your pond. Pocostomous will thrive in warmer climates, but those of you who live in the cooler climates up north where you see hard freezes, bring in your pocostomus inside in early fall, or they will die of exposure.
D. **Water hyacinth and water lettuce** are a floating subtropical plant. If you live in Florida or Hawaii, you do not want water hyacinth in your ponds as they can get very invasive in those climates. In cooler areas, they are great, because they provide shade for your fish and also help consume the carbon dioxide in your water created by your fish.
E. **Water lilies, water irises, and other pond plants** will consume fish excrement and decaying solid biological matter with their root system, acting as a natural filter.

Pond fish come in many varieties from the exotic to the mundane, but there is something for everyone. Most of the popular pond fish are in the carp family as a form of some kind of decorative carp. Decorative carp are basically domesticated breeds of carp which are bred for their color and beauty. Some of the larger ponds can also be stocked with game fish as well. Because this ebook is primarily dedicated to the basic homeowner and do-it-yourselfer, we will primarily deal with the basic pond fish which can be found everywhere. Different members of the carp family bred for ponds and their subspecies are listed below.

A. **Goldfish** are the most common of the decorative carp family. Goldfish come in a variety of color and have the typical body of a carp. Goldfish can come in bright reds, oranges, yellows, or even in browns and blacks. Types of goldfish subspecies are listed below
   1. **Comets** are long slender goldfish which have that traditional fish shape. You can get pool comets at any pet shop for five to ten dollars a fish. There is a better and cheaper alternative to getting comets. Go to the pets department at Walmart, Petsmart, or Petco. You will see they sell piranhas. Typically, people who feed piranhas, they will feed them baby goldfish. These are known as feeder fish and are very small. Sometimes, you can get them for as cheap as ten cents a bag or five cents per fish, depending on the store you go. They may be too small for your liking, but they are the best test fish, as they are cheap. Because goldfish are carp, they will grow big, so before you know it, they can get as big as koi.
   2. **Fantails** are also in the goldfish family. These are fairly small when you buy them at the pet shop, but they can get big too. Fantails are a very beautiful addition to your pond. They can come in a variety of colors from bright red and orange to calico colors. Fantails have a round body and a long butterfly like tail which is almost as long as its body. They literally look like little butterflies in the water.
B. **Shubunkins** are not goldfish, but they are in the carp family. Unlike most carp, shubunkins will not grow more than six inches long. Shubunkins have the body of a comet goldfish and a tail and fins of a fantail. They do not usually come in red, but there may be some varieties which are red. Typically, shubunkins come in a range of red, blue, black, and silver spots all

over its body. They are very beautiful fish and dart across your pond showing off their beautiful bodies.

C. **Koi** are a hybridized variety of the Chinese river carp. Originally bred in Japan by Buddhist and Shinto priests for the meditation ponds of their temples, koi are very expensive and known for their size and color. The koi is a close cousin of the Chinese river carp, which is considered to be an invasive species of carp in some areas, so you might need to check with the DNR of your state to find out regulations on raising koi in your ponds. In places which are flood prone and have problems with the Chinese river carp may not allow koi in outdoor ponds for fear they might escape into the river ecosystem if the pond gets submerged in a flood. Koi are very beautiful fish, but they are very high maintenance. They can also get very large, sometimes outgrowing your pond, so it is a good idea to have a large pond with a minimum of a ten foot width and twenty foot length for koi to have enough room. There are different varieties of koi listed below.

1. **The rising sun koi** is a koi which is all white and has a bright red dot by its dorsal fin, looking like it's wearing the Japanese flag, hence its name.

2. **The doitsu** is actually a cross between the Japanese koi and the German leather carp. Doitsu koi are different as they have a leathery skin, like the German leather carp, but they have a bluish color to them. Doitsu do not have scales on them as other koi do.

3. **The butterfly koi** is a variety of koi that was originally not bred in Japan. In fact the butterfly koi were originally bred in the US by hybridizing the Japanese koi with fantail goldfish. When the embryo were hybridized, the fish grows large, like most koi do. Also, the body of the butterfly koi has the same shape as other koi do. The difference is in the fins. Butterfly koi have very large side and tale fins which sway and flutter around as it swims about the pond. Though not popular in Japan, these koi are very beautiful and can be wonderful addition to your pond. Butterfly koi come in a variety of colors from bright reds and whites to calico color.

4. **Standard koi** are basically like oversized goldfish with whiskers. This is the difference between koi and goldfish. Koi have whiskers on the edges of their mouths and goldfish do not. This comes from their cousin, the Chinese river carp. Standard koi come in red, white, brown, orange, and yellow. You can also get standard koi with multiple colors, such as red and black, orange and black, calico, and other varieties.

D. **German leather carp** are harder to find, but you might find them in specialty shops which deal in more exotic pond fish. Originally bred in Germany for food, the German leather carp is brown in color and has a leathery skin with no scales. They can get fairly large, so you should have a large pond for this fish. Some German leather carp can get bigger than koi.

Prevention of predators is key when stocking your pond with fish. Depending on which area you live in, there are many predatory animals which can decimate all the fish in your pond relatively quick if you are not vigilant. Depending in areas where you are at, some of the most common predators are listed below.

A. **Domestic and ferrel cats** are the biggest problem for pond fish nationwide. You need to take extra precautions in keeping cats away from your fishpond. Any area where people have cats as pets could also have a population of ferrel cats. Ferrel cats are cats which were originally domestic, but may have been abandoned or thrown away as kittens, so they became wild. Ferrel cats do multiply, so areas where ferrel cats are a problem, extra care is needed in keeping the cats away from your pond. Cats typically will catch your fish if they have a shallow entry into your pond. Steep banks around your entire pond and a good six inches to a foot from the rim of your pond to the water level is the best way to keep cats away from your fish. Cats, in general, hate water and hate to get wet, so they will fear falling into the water. You can also use sharp jagged stones cemented to the rim of your pond which can make it uncomfortable for cats to sit at the water's edge and prevent them to position themselves in an effective position for catching fish.

B. **Raccoons** are common all over the lower 48 states, and they can be just as bad a predator as cats. Like cats, raccoons do not like to jump into the water and get wet. Raccoons like a shallow slope into the water and will simply kill the fish with a stroke of their claws. Raccoons have difficulty balancing themselves on steeper concrete banks of a pond. Like with cats, having a steep or vertical bank that goes down six inches to one foot before the water level is the most effective way to keep raccoons at bay.

C. **Snapping turtles** are rather large and common in the Midwest. Snapping turtles are happy in water and will eat your fish. The problem with snapping turtles is that they will sneak in your pond quietly and at night. If one gets in your pond, your fish are gonners. Care needs to be taken when handling a snapping turtle and the best way to deal with them is to call animal control. Snapping turtles have a strong beak and are capable of taking off a fingure, so do not get your hands close to its head. Also, snapping turtles do get very aggressive and will snap at you if you get too close to them.

D. **Great blue herons,** common in the Midwest and central states during the summer and in Florida in the winter, can be a major problem. You cannot kill this bird as it is an endangered species, but they will decimate your pond. These large migratory birds look beautiful but the best way to keep them from getting into your pond is to have a decoy. This usually keeps them away as they think it is a rival.

E. **King fishers** are a small freshwater bird which has a white breast, blue wings, orange collar, and a straight pointed black beak. These birds are common all over the US and Canada and they will dive into your pond and catch your fish for a quick snack. Use extra caution if you live near a lake or river, as those are areas where king fishers are likely to be around. The best way to prevent king fishers from coming to your pond is by listening for its call. It is a short high pitch fluttering whistling sound, similar to a police whistle. King fishers are rather elusive birds, so they can be difficult to repel. Sometimes, if king fishers are a serious problem, you may need to have bird netting over your pond.

F. **Otters** are mainly in the Northwest and in Canada. Otters typically like rivers, but they are fish eaters and could find an easy meal in your pond. Because otters are river animals, they like shallow banks in which they can launch themselves in the water. Steep sides with a low water level can keep the otter from getting out of your pond. You then can catch it and it will be a trauma for it and will not come back.

G. **Bears** in the eastern US states of Pennsylvania, Tennessee, North Carolina, West Virginia, and Virginia or in the Rockies out west can be a serious problem. If you see a bear in your pond, do not confront it yourself. Call animal control to have it removed. Bears are very dangerous and can kill with a swipe of their claws.

H. **Mountain lions** are in the cat family and may want to have one of your prize koi as a snack. Again, mountain lions are encroaching in subdivisions from the Rockies to the central states. These large cats can be very aggressive, so call animal control if you see them near your pond.

Underwater caverns are things you can incorporate in your pond construction to help your fish hide from predators. If you go the masonry rout when building your pond, you can actually create curved caverns which fish can go deep into and be inaccessible to predators reach. Also, for a loose rock construction, you can make fish caves with old clay piping and place them in between heavy stones which a predatory animal cannot move to access the hiding place.

Proper biological treatments need to be observed over the course of the year. As mentioned above, you can get biological solutions from companies, like EcoLabs, Microbelift in particular. When we had our service, we often used Microbelift products for our ponds, as they did a very good job from removing sludge to keeping the water clear and even curtailing the mosquito population around the pond. Some of the biological treatments which should be done seasonally are listed below.

A. **Spring** is when it all starts. This is when your fish will spawn and when all dead plant matter which has accumulated during the late fall and winter begins to decay into sludge. Your fish will hibernate during the winter and won't move much until it gets warmer. You do not want to feed fish until the water temperature reaches the upper sixties Fahrenheit. Before then, fish do not really eat and won't digest much of the food, so you will have a big excrement problem. Fish typically produce little excrement unless they are overfed. This is why fish should only be fed once a day or every other day. They'll have plenty of natural food, such as insects, algae, and more, so they won't starve if you don't feed them for over a week. Now when feeding starts is also when you want to start biologically treating your pond, which can be from late March to early May, depending on where you live. Biological treatment recommended for spring is listed below.

   1. **Sludge Away** is a biological solution in the Microbelift product line, but other brands have similar solutions. This is a special bacteria which will remove any sludge and decaying plant matter from the fall and winter. This solution will reek like stagnant water or raw sewage, but it is harmless to your fish and does a good job. There is a course of treatment with Sludge Away or like solutions. The color of the solution is black, but it will not turn your water black. The reason is that this is a bacteria which eats away at some of the most stubborn sludge and so it is grown in a type of sludge in a laboratory. The course of treatment for Sludge Away should go for six weeks as the weather starts getting warmer. The bacteria will be active when the water temperature is as low as 40 degrees Fahrenheit.

   2. **Enzyme packets** are made both by Microbelift and other biological companies. These enzymes are a light brown powder and will activate when in contact with water. These enzymes work very well in dissolving dead leaves which do not disintegrate fast. This is necessary where you have oaks or pines. These come in packets of a water-soluble cellulose plastic, which will dissolve in contact with the water. When beginning the Sludge removal treatment, add some of these enzymes with the first treatment.

B. **Summer** is a season where everything is active. The fish are actively swimming around the pond, grabbing pieces of fish food, insects, or other things that fall in the pond. Some plant material may fall or blow into the pond, dead flower pedals, seeds, acorns (late summer), etc. During the summertime, you mainly want to maintain your pond's ecosystem. There are biological solutions specifically for the summer months. Microbelift and like brands have a special bacterial solution which is a brownish color in the bottle, but these bacteria will consume the particulates which can cause the water to become murky, and keep fish excrement under control by consuming all necrotic matter and excreted matter in the pond. This bacteria together with snails and freshwater clams or muscles can keep your pond's ecosystem healthy and your fishpond enjoyable all summer long.

C. **Fall** is a time when leaves can fill up your pond at lightning speed. They come down from the trees and land in the water along with more leaves being blown into the pond by wind or careless blowing of leaves into the ponds. Try not to blow in the direction of your pond when cleaning leaves from your lawns and flowerbeds. Leaves can be a problem as they can make the water too acid and they are difficult to fish out. You can use the same enzyme packs which you use in spring to help break down the leaf matter in your pond. Add that with a healthy dose of Sludge Away or like solution and by November or December, you will have gotten a head start in getting rid of those stinky leaves from your pond. As long it does not get below freezing for a long period of time, the bacteria in Sludge Away and the enzymes will work at breaking down any dead matter in the water.

D. **Winter** is a season which nothing should be done, as everything is frozen and nothing is active.

Proper stocking your pond with fish can guarantee your fish will last for a ling time. When you buy your fish for your pond, you don't want to simply throw them into the water when you bring them home. When you buy pond fish, they will be in a plastic bag with water, just like when you buy aquarium fish. You need to place the fish bag in the water of your pond and let the water temperature in the bag get to be the same as the temperature of the pond. This will acclimate the fish and they will not have shock. It usually takes ten minutes for your new fish to get acclimated, then carefully open the bag and release them into the pond.

Water Features for your Pond
With ponds, you will need movement of water for aeration. You can do this by adding water features, such as a cascade, waterfall, or fountain-like features. The different water features will be discussed in this section. You can also use some of these in freestanding pieces and not connect them to a pond if a fishpond is not your cup of tea.

Building a waterfall is one of the easiest water features you can build for your pond. These are very nice and they look natural. The key in building a successful waterfall or cascade is to use pond rubber and chickenwire for mortaring. You can also get waterproof goop which you can squeeze and pack into the cracks between the slabs of flagstone to keep water from leaking out of the pond system. Simply run the piping from the filter box connected to the pump to the head of the waterfall and adjust the flow control on the manifold, especially if you have multiple water features. See Figure Four below.

Figure Four: Construction and water flow of a waterfall or cascade.

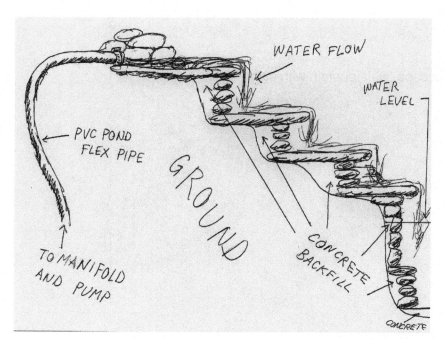

Hardscaping is the art of using mortaring and masonry to create water features which can either be a statue or wall fountains. The easiest hardscape you can create is a wall fountain with a catch basin. If you incorporate this with your fishpond, you can then let the catch basin drain into the pond through a rock feature to create a multiple waterfall. See Figures Five and Six below.

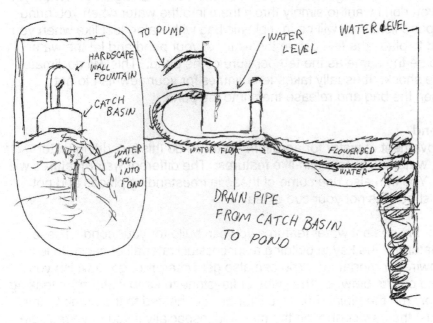

Figure Five: An example of hardscaping for your fishpond.

Figure Six: Standalone hardscape, wall fountain with catch basin

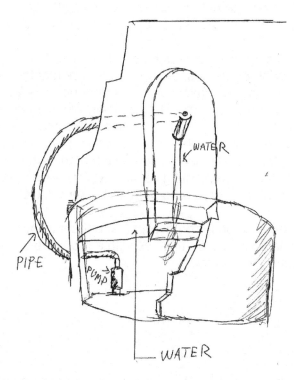

Rills are actually a Middle Eastern water feature which can be linked with hardscaping. A rill is a narrow stream of water which is imbedded in your patio. Another neat idea if you like to build a rectangular reflecting pond, having wall fountains or a pedestal fountain with water draining from the catch basins into rills which then lead them into the pond.

A bog garden is another water feature you can build. Bog gardens are very easy to build and you can incorporate them into your fishpond or you can have just a bog garden. Bog gardens may be too small and too dense for fish, but they can attract frogs which also make a pleasant sound during the summer.

A bog garden is basically a man-made swamp. Simply have a wet shallow area which can trap water and it is ideal for growing fancy large water plants, such as canna lilies, elephant ears, water iris, and more.

Water Plants
To have a healthy water garden with fish, you should have a variety of water plants also. You want to take note, that if you have koi, you will have to feed them regularly to keep them from destroying your water plants. Koi are the literal vandals and will chew on every plant they come in contact with. Goldfish are not as destructive in that respect. Below is a list of common water plants which you can have for your pond, bog garden, or both.

A. **Water lilies** are the most common water plant for your pond. These are where the classic lilypad comes from. These are beautiful but they do need sun. Their blooms go from mid May all the way to mid September, so you will have floral beauty floating on those round green saucer-shaped leaves all summer long. Flowers from water lilies can range from pinks and purples to reds and whites. Water lilies grow out of a tuber, so you will need to get an underwater planter, which is a porous container and place it in sand and pea gravel to weigh it down to the bottom of the pond. Do not use soils or fertilizers for water lilies as they can cause an algae boom in your pond. You can get fertilizer pegs which slowly dissolve in the sand and pea gravel mix of the plant, but use the pegs sparingly and read the instructions for proper use.

B. **Water iris** look like regular iris and their flowers are the same and have the same colors. The leaves of water iris are just like the leaves of regular iris, but are more thick together. Water iris are great for both your bog garden or on the shallow edges of your pond. Water iris do spread, so you want to give them some growing room. They typically blossom in late May to early June. Water iris have bulb like roots which need to be planted like water lilies.

C. **Elephant ears** are more a tropical plant and need either to be brought in during the winter months or be replaced in the summer. These plants are also known as taros and grow enormous leaves in the shape of elephant ears. These plants give your water garden that tropical feel and can get massive. They grow out of a tuber and need to be kept in water at all times.

D. **Canna lilies** are also annuals and are wonderful for both bog gardens and the shallow areas of your pond. These plants have very large and broad leaves with a red flower. They grow out of a tuber and can be brought in during the winter.

Low Maintenance Water Features

Like water features but are on a budget? Well, this segment is for you. Maybe, you just want to be lazy and want to hear the relaxing sound of water and not do all the work maintaining it. Well, low maintenance water features do not require any maintenance or filters. Just a pump, fountain head, and pipe. Types of fountains you can build are listed below.

Before we get into the different types of fountains, however, we would like to write about the typical garbage can construction. This is the easiest DIY fountain project to build. All you need to do is get a large 32 gallon plastic garbage can or if you want a large fountain with a loud splash, get a plastic 55 gallon fire barrel at a farm supply store, like Rural King, Tractor Supply, or Big R, which sell large items of this nature for farmers.

The basic construction is very simple, however, if you live in a climate with a hard freeze, you will want to drain the container to prevent the pump and the container from cracking as the water freezes. You will want to burry the plastic container into the ground and if you like the fountain to be elevated a bit, then burry the garbage can until about six inches stick up above the ground. You can then mortar stone around the rim of the garbage can so it will not show. Then construct a cover which has several layers of chickenwire over pipe with room for the pipe holding the fountain head to go through. This is your basic cover which hides the garbage can and the components of the pump. You can cover the chickenwire framed structure with pebbles which you can find at any landscape center or stone yard. See Figure Seven below to see how a garbage can fountain can be constructed with relative ease.

Figure Seven: The typical garbage can fountain construction

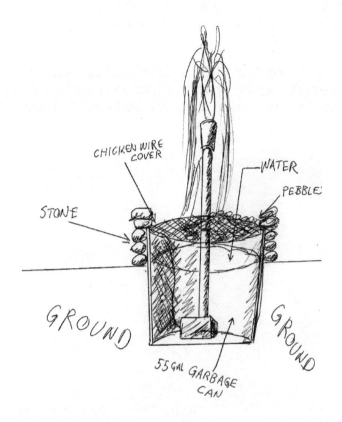

CHICKEN WIRE COVER

STONE

WATER

PEBBLE

GROUND

GROUND

55 GAL GARBAGE CAN

Different water features can be created with a garbage can fountain. These features are covered below. You can get the different fountain heads at any pond specialty shop or you can even make some yourself by drilling holes in pipes for water to come out.

A. **Geyser fountains** are the easiest to construct. These simply require a pipe to come out of the pump and simply let the water shoot up. To have a large geyser, get a plastic fire bucket and a powerful pump, you can have an amazing geyser with loud splash.

B. **Throffer fountains** have a fountain head which has a special opening that allows the water to throf and makes a low geyser like spray, also causes a loud splash.

C. **Bell fountains** are very common and a bell head can even be found in the seasonal departments of big home improvement stores, like Lowe's or Home Depot. Very easy to construct and cause the water to make a bell shape. With lighting features, you can have some amazing affects at night.

D. **Spray and tiered fountains** are fountain heads which have holes and the water comes out of the different holes. Some look like inverted multitiered shower heads which spray water in a classical fountain pattern. You can also get creative with this by creating your own spray fountain and with a powerful enough pump, you can have an amazing effect with low cost.

Making Complex Water Features
If you are looking to make a water garden which is the talk of the block, then you can do this by having a large pond, with several different pumps and special manifolds to control the flow. Use all the information above to create the water features you like, but you want to make sure if you run several water features off of one pump, you want to have a pump which can pump out 3,000

to 6,000 gallons per hour. These are some of the larger and more expensive pumps, but they are well worth the money. It is always better to get a pump which is much stronger than you need. It gives you more water flow to play with.

Creating a water manifold is very simple. Simply get PVC piping and cement, water valves, which can be adjustable by small increments, a hose spicket, incase you have to drain the pond, and beaded connectors to attach the flex pipes to pump and filters and different water features.   See Figure Eight below.

Figure Eight: Typical manifold construction

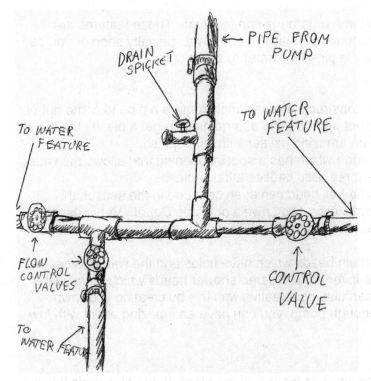

Water gardens can be the jewel in the crown when it comes to landscaping your yard. The sound of the water flowing is tranquil and can be a great relief at the end of a stressful day and you can also enjoy watching the fish with your children. Water gardens are also pleasant to be around when with friends and the relaxing sound of water can also help you sleep on those warm summer nights with the windows open.

Epilogue

Now that you have learned how to build the yard of your dreams, you need to know some basic maintenance tips.

You will be spending more time maintaining your landscaping than building and designing it. Proper maintenance goes beyond mowing the lawn, weeding, or doing other things around the yard. Your pond needs maintenance and even masonry needs maintenance, such as tuck pointing.

Now that you have come this far, you will learn some methods on mowing, fertilizing, and treating your lawn. You will also learn how to keep pesky animals, such as deer, groundhogs, and other animals from ravaging your prize landscape plants.

Proper Lawn Maintenance
The most temperamental and the most high maintenance in any ordinary landscaping project, besides water gardens, is your lawn. In fact, it is because of the high maintenance involved that many people are getting away from lawns and wanting to go more to rock gardens and bushes and mulch, though they have their maintenance issues too.

Mowing is the major part of lawn maintenance. Grass is a plant which thrives in moisture, but will survive in droughts. This means that when it rains frequently, the grass will grow quickly and will need to be cut every week or sometimes twice every week. Here is the tricky part. Unless you have a high quality mower with a vacuum and mulching fan, you always want to mow the lawn when it is as dry as possible. This is because wet grass can stick to the bottom of your mowing deck, gum up your blades and drive belts. Wet grass, as it's cut, will also collect and stick to the bottom of your mowing deck, causing your mower to clump and can also make the engine of the mower work harder, thus lessens the life of your mower and its parts. An overworking engine can cause a fire or a blown gasket in your mower.

This obviously is a problem if it rains every day. One idea is that if there is constant rain in the forecast, if you have a day of dry weather before the next rain, then use a push blower that you would use for leaves to blow the lawn two to three times to dry the grass, then mow.

Mulching versus bagging is a question which everyone has to ask. It may be easier to mulch your grass, but the reality is that mulching may not be the best thing you can do for your lawn. If you mulch your lawn, then you can have a problem with collecting thatch and that can make thatching your lawn more difficult in the spring. Furthermore, if you mulch when the grass is wet, you will have unsightly clumps which will have to be picked up right after you have mowed.

Bagging is much healthier for your lawn and the grass clippings will decompose very quickly in your compost bin. Sometimes, if you have a lawn mower with a narrow chute, the crass clippings can clog the chute and you will have clumps which you will have to pick up. Wet grass can clog bag chutes in smaller mowers rather quickly. Bagging takes longer than mulching, but in the long run, you will have a greener lawn.

Mowing height is also critical. Typically, most lawns are mowed at about two and a half inches high. Some people like a higher cut and others like a lower cut. Golf courses will have their grass cut at one and a half inch and the greens even lower. We don't recommend mowing that low as most soils can be soft and you can risk scalping your lawn, leaving unsightly holes of dirt in your lawn. Ideally cut at two and a half inches. If you cut higher than that, your lawn will get higher faster and if you cut lower, you could harm your lawn.

When to mow can depend on you and your personal tastes. However, when you notice your lawn begins to have that shaggy look and the grass looks uneven and wild, then it's time to mow. Try not to wait until the grass goes to seed. Then it can get more difficult to mow.

When is the right season to mow? Typically, mowing season begins when the weather gets warmer and you have frequent rain showers. In most of the US and Canada, mowing season typically begins in late April and goes on to early October, before the leaves begin to fall. Further north in Canada and Alaska, mowing season may go from late May to early September.

When is it time to fertilize? Typically, in the spring, after the first mowing of the season, you should fertilize the lawn and give it that shot in the arm. You should then fertilize it with a good helping of water in the middle of the summer when rain is more scarce. Typically, there are two rainy seasons. Early to mid spring into early summer and then late summer into early fall. Fertilizing in mid summer is a good idea as the lawn will be relying on artificial watering from a hose or sprinkler system more often and the weather will be much hotter, thus your lawn will endure more stress. Naturally, during mid summer, most wild grasses stop growing and will dry out and begin to turn brown. You want to prevent this from happening. Fertilize again with winterization in mid October around your last mowing for the season.

Winterizing Sprinkler Systems and Water Features
If you have a sprinkler system for your lawn or a pond or water fountain with complex water features, you will want to winterize the system to keep water from staying in the pipes and

breaking them when it freezes in the winter. This is easily done with an air compressor and blowing the pipes with compressed air after unscrewing the connection to the source of water. With water features, you will want to drain catch basins and cover them up in the winter to keep rain and show from accumulating in them, then melting and turning into ice. The compressed air will clean all the pipes and keep them empty during the winter. Freezing temperatures and pipes broken to freezing is the main cause for expensive repairs.

Propagation of Annuals
As mentioned in Chapter One, you are able to propagate some annuals, such as coleus and impatients. Simply use mason sand and rooting powder and let grow. Begin this in late August. Get some growth lamps and have a growing area with the growth lamps set on a timer to mimics summer sun and your annuals will thrive inside during the winter. Water frequently.

Looking for Fish Disease
Having a fishpond can be a wonderful thing, but they are high maintenance. Fish, especially, need care. As mentioned in Chapter Seven, there is important care for fish, but sometimes fish can get diseases. This doesn't happen often, but it can happen. Listed below are common fish diseases and how to treat them.

A. **Ick** is a common disease which affects most varieties of carp, including goldfish and koi. Ick is a highly contagious fish disease which has white textured spots on the fish's fins and tails, then expanding to over take its body. If you notice one of your fish has developed ick, take it out of the pond and place it in a hospital or quarantine tank. There are medications available to treat ick and you can find them at Petsmart, Petco, or any other pet shop which specializes in fish. Watch all the other fish in the pond to see if any others develop the disease. If they do, then take them out too. Use care and place them in another quarantine tank with fresh water once you have seen the ick symptoms disappear. Keep the infected fish quarantined for a month before releasing them back into the pond.
B. **Fin and tail rot** is typically a fungal infection of a fish and it causes the fins and tail of your fish to rot and fall off. This can be treated in its early stages by isolating the infected fish and treating it with medicines. If the disease progresses, you may have to euthanize the fish.

Though the causes of these diseases is not known, monitor your fish. Feed them the healthy way and also watch for wounds. If a fish has a bleeding wound from an animal or having been attacked by another fish, take it out of the pond and treat it in a hospital tank.

Be Creative
In this last paragraph of the epilogue, you should be creative with your landscaping. Many landscaping stores and home improvement warehouse stores, such as Lowe's and Home Depot have a wide variety of books on the topic with designs, ideas, and different layouts to work from. If you have not done any landscaping before and you have your first house with a yard, it is understandable that you may want to copy everything by the book, but if you do that, you will have a cookie-cutter yard like everyone else. Be creative. Get the books for ideas. You can also subscribe to particular magazines. Some include Better Homes and Gardens which you can find at the cash register at almost every grocery store.

Think outside the box and look at other things besides the landscaping magazines and books. Other books to look at include encyclopedias with many pictures, picture books of foreign countries or areas within the US and Canada, and more. If you are a traveler, then the possibilities are endless. Pay attention to every detail you see in stonework, flower and plant arrangements, and take that into your landscaping.

Having the landscape you want can be the most fulfilling thing you can do for yourself. Your home and garden are your personal space. Make sure that you are happy with your design. Good luck!

CPSIA information can be obtained
at www.ICGtesting.com
Printed in the USA
LVOW03s1602280416
485769LV00013B/395/P

INGRAM
MAY 0 2 2016

9 781512 176285